Wicked Hartford

Wicked HARTFORD

STEVE THORNTON

THE History PRESS

Published by The History Press
Charleston, SC
www.historypress.net

Front cover, clockwise from upper left: public domain; www.Nihilist.fm, public domain; The Baseball Reliquary, public domain; public domain; public domain; public domain; public domain; public domain; George Grantham Bain Collection, Library of Congress; Digital Public Library of America, public domain; Cultusillusion collection, public domain.
Back cover: all images in the public domain.

First published 2017

Manufactured in the United States

ISBN 9781467137348

Library of Congress Control Number: 2017945008

For Megan, Pepper, Matt and Kate

CONTENTS

FOREWORD

Conniving bosses, predatory slumlords, greedy industrialists and political intrigue; every city has its wicked side, but not every city has a proper critic to chronicle it.

In Steve Thornton, the city of Hartford, Connecticut, has found its muckraker. As a labor organizer, people's historian and longtime rabble-rouser, Thornton has seen the wicked side of Hartford and lived to write about it.

Uncovering stories from the picket lines, prison files and dusty state archives, Thornton lays bare the sordid history of this seemingly staid insurance capital. From the slave insurrections of the seventeenth century to the dark excesses of the Gilded Age, through the pitched social battles of the 1960s and 1970s, no wicked deed goes unnoted in *Wicked Hartford.*

In loving detail, Thornton remaps the city, locating its rollicking beer halls, crowded opium dens and casinos of yesteryear as well as the notorious jails, poor houses and smallpox quarantines that have long since disappeared or been burned to the ground.

Turning city lore on its head, Thornton takes aim at the city's favored sons, questioning, for example, the character of Samuel Colt and the death-dealing firearms that were manufactured in Hartford and branded with his name. Describing the global impact of Hartford's major industry, Thornton quotes Mark Twain: "The fact is we make guns, and load them, and mean business."

Both scintillating and sympathetic, Thornton maintains his focus on the lives of workers and ordinary people. While lambasting slavery supporters, local fascists and heartless city fathers, he heralds the city's unsung heroes like the abolitionist Reverend James Pennington, suffragist Katharine Houghton Hepburn and Black Panther Butch Lewis, giving them their due for fighting the city's wickedness.

I am proud to write this foreword for Steve Thornton. Whether speaking in my classes on history panels or at large community forums, I have seen this man breathe new life into Hartford's history, giving people back their dignity in hope for a less wicked future.

CHRISTINA HEATHERTON
Trinity College

ACKNOWLEDGEMENTS

The names of many of the people who have inspired me are lost to history, but their struggles and victories should not be forgotten.

Friends and comrades who have encouraged my work include Peter Kellman, Nancy Chance, E. San Juan and Delia Aguilar. Andy Paiscik and Eugene Leach have been especially supportive.

I am deeply grateful to the folks at ConnecticutHistory.org (a project of Connecticut Humanities), *Connecticut Explored*, the Connecticut Historical Society and the Bridgeport History Center at the Bridgeport Public Library.

And not to be forgotten are the hardworking library staff at the Hartford and West Hartford Public Libraries, Hartford History Center, the Tamiment Library at NYU and the Schomberg Center for Research in Black Culture.

1

PROSTITUTION, THE SOCIAL EVIL

The "Ladies and Gents Dining Room and Cafe" advertised home cooking as its specialty. But if you walked into this Hartford establishment in 1912, there were no meals. The café was packed with prostitutes and the men who sought them. City officials called it "commercialized vice," flesh peddling transformed into a big business.

"Houses of ill fame" were well known to the Hartford public. With names like Kate Pratt's, Hub Smith's and Hunter's Place, these brothels existed mostly in the poor Front Street neighborhood, but not exclusively. Cadwell's was located on Woodland Street in Asylum Hill, not far from the respectable Nook Farm homes of Mark Twain and Harriet Beecher Stowe.

At the start of the twentieth century, prostitution could be found on the blocks between Commerce and Potter Streets to Ferry and State Streets. This was the oldest part of the city's east side, along the Connecticut River. Some city officials thought they could contain the "social evil" into one proscribed area. They figured this way the police could segregate the population and isolate the health risks.

Yet prostitutes were also active in many other areas of Hartford: the train station, private apartments and rooms, cafés and restaurants, theaters, hotels and roadhouses. Waiters and bartenders frequently became pimps, keeping a close eye on the money earned by their "humps," as they called the prostitutes. Women usually serviced between fifteen and twenty-five men a night.

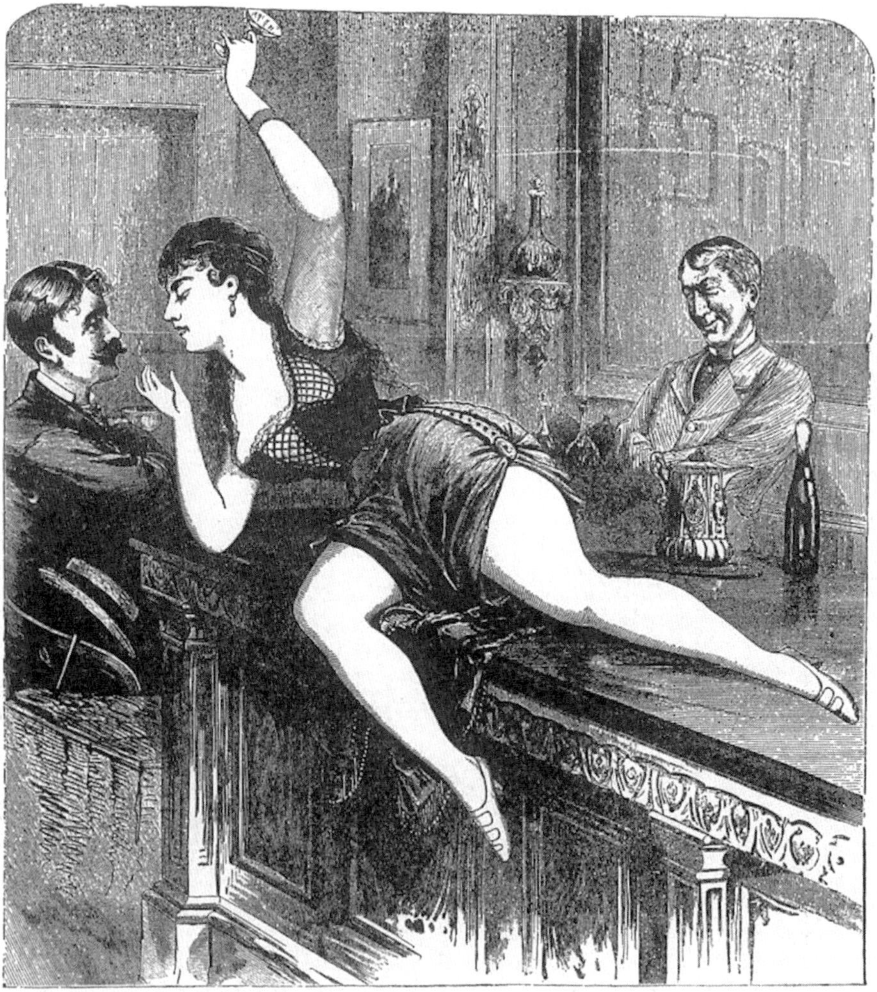

Nineteenth-century prostitute. *Cultusillusion collection.*

One of the most infamous bawdy-house owners was a federal detective from New York known as Pigniuolo. In Hartford, he owned a "fifty cent house." Although the detective was arrested and brought to trial, the all-male jury did not convict him.

HIDDEN DISEASE UNCOVERED

From 1908 to 1912, arrests of Hartford women dramatically increased. Breach of peace arrests jumped from 21 to 75 during that time. Fornication arrests increased from 4 to 20 women. Arrests for drunkenness rose from 197 to 439 cases.

Studies of the problem covered all aspects of female prostitution, but when it came to male prostitutes, the officials were clearly flummoxed: "The most disgusting and repulsive form in which [sexual perversion] manifests itself is in the male prostitute, who not only takes the place of the prostitute in fact, but even impersonates or resembles a female in his mannerism, voice and conversation....Four of these are men of wealth and social standing....Their practices are too revolting for discussion in this report."

In 1911, Hartford Hospital figures estimated that almost three hundred women were treated for illnesses that actually had a venereal origin. These included not just gonorrhea and syphilis (the cause of which was only discovered in 1906), but also eye diseases, miscarriages and brain tumors.

The double standard faced by Hartford women was nowhere more apparent than with the treatment of venereal disease. Doctors often lied to their female patients who had been infected with VD. As a 1913 Hartford Vice Commission report stated: "No good could possibly come by telling a wife that her enfeebled health since marriage was due to a venereal disease contracted by her husband perhaps years prior to their marriage, or that the same is the probable reason that their marriage has been childless. There is trouble enough in this world without adding more."

Not everyone agreed with the cover-up. Dr. Thomas Hepburn was one of the physicians who treated women with venereal disease at Hartford Hospital. There he saw firsthand how women's health was ravaged and how their infants suffered from these preventable diseases. This moved him to conclude that the statistics needed to be publicized and women needed to be educated.

Dr. Hepburn's wife concurred. She was Katharine Houghton Hepburn, a leading suffragist (and the mother of the famous actress). Along with her sister suffragists, including Hartford's Josephine Bennett, they reproduced and sold the vice commission report that had exposed the problems for the first time. Josephine's husband, Martin Toscan Bennett, was a member of the commission of twelve men and two women.

Apparently, it was not the intention of the commission to widely publicize its findings. Despite the fact that the city council had voted to create the study, it never voted to approve it.

This did not stop the early feminists from continuing to promote reproductive health services for women. Within a decade, they had invited Margaret Sanger to Hartford and together started one of the first Planned Parenthood groups. Hartford women like Hepburn and Bennett also organized the first birth control clinic in the state. Despite the condemnation of the local Catholic Church, the clinic provided lifesaving help to all women, including immigrants and the city's poorest families.

THE EARLIEST EXAMPLES

Ann Dunn and Caroline McElroy were unceremoniously escorted to the Hartford police station, where they were charged with prostitution. The arrest of the two women came in the summer of 1864 after a raid on two North Main Street brothels.

The owners and their families were not treated so harshly: Lyman Waters was released on a bond and a promise to "keep the peace"; Martha Ford received a suspended sentence. Ford's daughters got warnings. The four male customers picked up in the raid (whose names were not given to the press) were released with some words of warning but without charges. Dunn and McElroy were sentenced to forty-five days in jail. So much for victimless crimes.

The world's oldest profession thrived in nineteenth-century Hartford. As in other U.S. cities, prostitution both prospered and declined, depending on the moral and economic climate in which women found themselves. Social reformers used various methods to rid Hartford of its brothels, but none of them got to the root of the problem.

It took radical women like Emma Goldman and Hartford union organizer Rebecca Weiner to identify and propose a cure for the sex trade—the same social and economic conditions that gave rise to prostitution and exist to this day.

THE TIDE OF IMMORALITY

In 1851, Hartford's freemen created a police court to provide a more effective method of dealing with the rapidly growing vice problem. Until that time, "inmates of a house of ill fame are arrested, tried and sentenced to the workhouse for thirty days. Yet in less than a week's time, the same individuals are again in the city pursuing their old avocations," complained the *Hartford Courant*. Without the new court powers, the newspaper argued, "All the police force in the world cannot suppress the tide of immorality that is setting upon us."

Although prostitution was often treated with less severity than other crimes, the consequences of arrest and conviction had grave outcomes for many of the women (and sometimes men) involved. In September 1860, Laura Peck was arrested for running a Front Street bordello. Facing humiliation and a criminal record, she tried to hang herself out of a window with her shawl. That attempt failed, so Peck tied a rope tightly around her throat. She was found on her jail bunk groaning in pain. The authorities saw her swollen neck and thought she had taken poison. They called in a doctor, who treated her with an antidote, but to no avail. Her strangulation, according to one press report, had been discovered too late.

One young man found himself in a Hartford court in 1850. He was a native of the city who had moved to Buffalo, New York, with his wife and young son. He prospered in business but returned to Hartford to aid his dying mother.

The young husband left his family in the care of a male friend. Upon his return, he found that his wife had eloped with the friend to a nearby city, abandoning their son.

The heartbroken husband's mental health quickly deteriorated; he started to drink and began to steal to support himself. After a month in jail, he visited a house of prostitution and was astonished to find his wife employed there, sitting "upon the lap of a disgusting ruffian," according to the news report.

Nelly Adams was arrested by Hartford police for being a "common prostitute" in the summer of 1862. She had apparently dated the son of a well-known Hartford citizen and upon her arrest sent word to have him bail her out. Unfortunately, the messenger gave the note to the young man's father, who showed up at the police station instead. "A scene ensued which we leave to the reader's imagination," the *Courant* reported.

In the mid-nineteenth century, the sex trade was so lucrative in the Northeast that it was exported to other parts of the country. An 1866 tragedy at sea underscored this expansion of the sex business. The steamer *Evening Star*, commanded by a Captain Knapp of Stamford, sank off the East Coast on its way south from New York. Among the three hundred souls who perished were ninety-seven New York prostitutes headed for work in New Orleans.

REFORM, RAIDS AND REMOVAL

As the twentieth century approached, the Hartford Charity Organization Society reported twelve brothels operating in the city, mostly in immigrant neighborhoods, employing at least four hundred women. In a city with a population of about fifty thousand, this equaled one prostitute for every thirty Hartford men.

Attempts to curb the trade varied. In the 1870s, moral crusaders tried the personal approach. Seeing prostitution as the function of individual weakness, local charities worked hard to show "degraded girls" the path to redemption. One group opened a public room on the city's east side so the women could be uplifted by live music. The effort solicited only a few customers and was soon closed. The reformers blamed their failure on the influence of rum and the girls' personal flaws.

In 1898, city reformers used the "ethnic cleansing" approach. Gold Street tenements, some of which housed brothels, were populated by mostly black and poor Irish families. After a campaign to clean up the neighborhood, the entire street was razed. The demolition succeeded in restoring the historic cemetery nearby, but it did nothing to stop prostitution. Increased legal scrutiny intensified in the period from 1907 to 1911. Spurred on by the Hartford clergy, the police stormed bordellos in well-publicized raids. As usual, the prostitutes were fined and jailed; the owners got out on bond and the johns were seldom, if ever, charged.

Hartford police had an ambivalent attitude toward the sex trade. Despite the fact that prostitution was clearly illegal, it was a source of income for local cops. A scandalous trial in 1911 exposed the financial connection between the police and whorehouse owners; it didn't take a genius to see that law enforcement looked the other way when the social reformers weren't watching.

Also in 1911, under pressure by civic groups, Hartford mayor Edward L. Smith closed all of the city's brothels. Two years later, the vice commission reported that the closures were successful. But the problem simply moved to the streets and spread throughout the city. One of the first acts of the new police vice squad was a sweep of local restaurants and cafés where streetwalkers congregated. When the local sex houses closed shop, women were forced out on their own, arguably more independent but also more isolated and vulnerable than when they operated under a common roof.

THE TIN PLATE ORDINANCE

Prescriptions for reform always targeted the working women involved in commercialized vice, but rarely the men or property owners. One exception was known as the "Tin Plate Ordinance," first established in Portland, Oregon. This law required each commercial building to attach a metal sign near the front door. The owner's and landlord's names would be clearly visible from the street. As the Hartford vice commission report explained:

> *We believe that such an ordinance would have a direct repressive action upon prostitution in this city. Its indirect influence would also be large, as it would make for a better enforcement of tenement house laws, laws respecting sanitation, and laws of all kinds concerning disorderly places.*
>
> *To take a concrete instance, a certain saloon in Hartford was noted during the months of our investigation as being used almost exclusively as a rendezvous for prostitutes, their pimps and patrons. The place was not on the East Side but on a street where it was quite conspicuous. It is fairly safe to assume that if the owner's name had been displayed over the door of that saloon the premises would never have been used as they were.*
>
> *In any event his attention would have been called so frequently to the disorderly acts taking place within that he could not plead ignorance. It is unlikely that he would have been willing to have it advertised that he was profiting as landlord by the pimp-owned girls operating within.*

This proposed city law was a double whammy for slumlords. Not only would their link to prostitution be exposed, but tenants would also know whom they could blame for their substandard living conditions. They could put direct pressure on the landowners. The law was never adopted.

TEMPTATION AND DEFILEMENT

On March 20, 1911, five days before the infamous Triangle Shirtwaist Factory fire that killed 146 workers in New York City, Hartford tailors took to the streets for better wages and safer working conditions. Their strike was triggered by the firing of Rebecca Weiner, a young organizer for the International Ladies' Garment Workers Union (ILGWU).

Rebecca had been organizing a union of the alteration tailors at the Sage Allen department store. When store owner Norman Allen found out, Rebecca was sacked. Twenty tailors walked out in protest. Allen shipped the strikers' unfinished work to G. Fox, Brown Thomson and other downtown stores. The two hundred tailors of those establishments refused to be strikebreakers and were locked out of their jobs.

Rebecca Weiner's organizing efforts did not just target the economic and safety conditions of the tailors; they also exposed the socially enforced options that young working women faced. Rebecca knew that Hartford garment laborers worked fifty-seven hours a week, long hours that produced wages half of what similar work paid in New York.

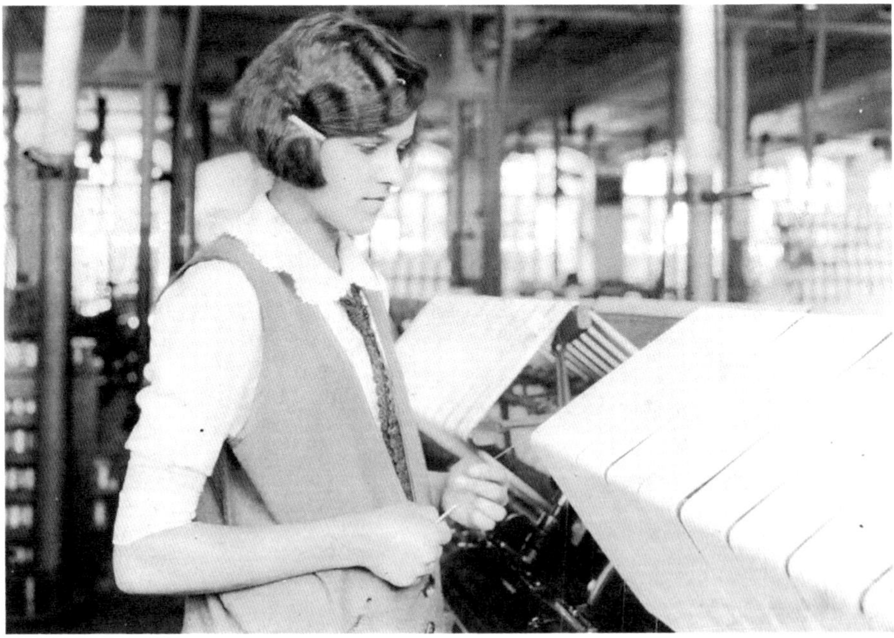

Young factory women were especially vulnerable to the advances of the foreman, and to street life. *Lewis Hine, National Child Labor Committee. Library of Congress.*

The six-day-a-week schedule meant that there was almost no time for a personal life outside of the workplace. Women workers were often prey for a male supervisor who had the power to fine them or withhold wages if they resisted his sexual advances. One vice commission story describes a typical situation: "[The young woman] was ruined by the superintendent of the mill where she worked. He was a married man. She was on piece work. He promised her better work if she would yield. Afterwards he gave her good yarn for a while and her wages were fine. His demands came oftener. She was finally caught with him and had to leave the mill. She came to Hartford but could not find any work, so she went on to the streets."

A federal Department of Labor study had already found nearly half the prostitutes surveyed had previously worked in factories and shops before turning tricks. "No working girl can ply her honest calling for less than $6 a week," Rebecca reported in the ILGWU newspaper, "and be safe from the temptation and defilement to which she is exposed in the polluting atmosphere that environs her struggle for decent living."

Norman Allen was a formidable foe, determined to thwart Rebecca Weiner's organizing efforts. Not only was he a wealthy capitalist, Allen also served as the head of the State Businessmen's Association and as a Hartford Police commissioner. This combination of legal, political and economic muscle was too much for the tailors in 1911.

LOVE, MARRIAGE AND CAPITALISM

Two years after the failed strike, five hundred people crowded into Hartford's Columbia Hall to hear "the most dangerous woman in America." Emma Goldman was an anarchist, a feminist and a speaker with a provocative message. When she wasn't in jail for "inciting to riot" or fundraising for imprisoned members of the militant Industrial Workers of the World (the Wobblies), Goldman was writing and speaking on behalf of the liberation of women.

On February 12, 1913, she spoke to the Hartford crowd on "Marriage and Love." Goldman had been widely condemned as an advocate of "free love," a notion that captured many intellectuals on the left and playwrights of the time but scandalized proper society.

"Free love? As if love is anything but free it can live in no other atmosphere," she told the enthusiastic audience. Marriage, on the other

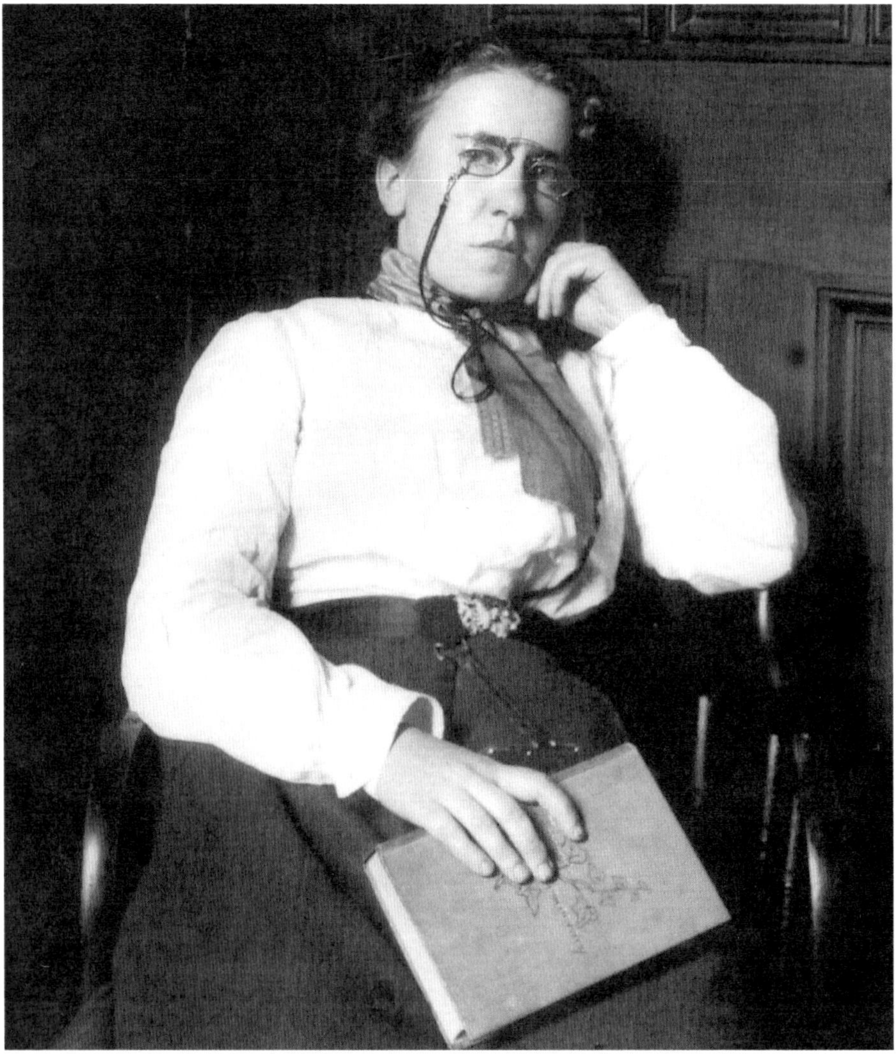

Emma Goldman, "the most dangerous woman in America." *www.Nihilist.fm.*

hand, "incapacitates a woman for life's struggle, annihilates her social consciousness, paralyzes her imagination."

Emma Goldman's ideas were considered so inflammatory that she spent much of her adult life being ostracized, forced at times to find shelter in local parks or brothels. Those experiences informed her later thinking on prostitution. *The Traffic in Women*, published in 1910, was her clear-headed analysis of why women ended up selling their bodies.

"What is really the cause of the trade in women?" Goldman wrote. "Exploitation, of course…it is merely a question of degree whether she sells herself to one man, in or out of marriage, or to many men." Goldman cited the studies of noted sociologists and Dr. William Sanger (husband of birth-control advocate Margaret Sanger) to prove her point: society's dominant social customs pressured young women either to marry or to sell sex to survive.

In 1900, 8,597 Hartford women were the sole support of their families. Most were between sixteen and twenty-four years of age. It was not just capitalism, however, that forced women into the profession. Goldman explained: "I refer to the sex question, the very mention of which causes most people moral spasms." Women are reared as a sex commodity, she argued, but are kept in the dark about adult sexual relations. No wonder they fell easy prey to prostitution and similar exploitative relationships.

Nothing less than a fundamental upheaval of traditional morality, Goldman concluded, along with the abolition of industrial slavery, could eradicate prostitution.

Hartford's city fathers, however, were no more likely to heed Emma Goldman's theories than they were to listen to the union demands of Rebecca Weiner.

"There's Money in It"

Strip away the excuses and rationales for prostitution and, at the core, is profit. As the Hartford commission report put it: "A considerable amount of the social evil is the creation of cold-blooded, commercial enterprise. Added to the prostitution arising inevitably from human weakness and misfortune is that which is built up as a business by middlemen who force a supply of girls to houses and stimulate a demand. There's money in it—profit in selling girls to houses, profit in selling their services, profit in selling clothes to them and liquor to their customers, profit in renting disorderly houses and apartments."

For two centuries, women have walked the Capital City's streets. Neither moralizing nor legal force has put an end to the sex workers' trade.

2

WICKED SAM COLT

What sort of businessman would Samuel Colt be considered today? He is well known as a manufacturing wizard and the original "pulled up by his bootstraps" success story. But this celebrated arms manufacturer has left a morally challenged legacy.

Interpreting the past is a tricky business, but there are some things we know for sure. Colt started his career by selling hits of nitrous oxide to curious audiences for a cheap high. Eventually, he became an army "colonel" who never saw battle, and he used bribery to secure lucrative government contracts.

Maybe worst of all, Colt sold weapons to both the North and the South in the arms buildup before the Civil War. He was called the "revolving patriot" by his critics.

THE LITTLE COLONEL

Sam Colt was described as an "autocratic maniac" who ran his operation like a southern plantation. "While Colt's workers were not legally enslaved, it was always more a matter of degree than kind," wrote historian William Hosley in *Colt: The Making of an American Legend*.

Colt's reputation was tarnished in other ways, as well. He used bribery to advance his business opportunities. Although he was acquitted of the charge

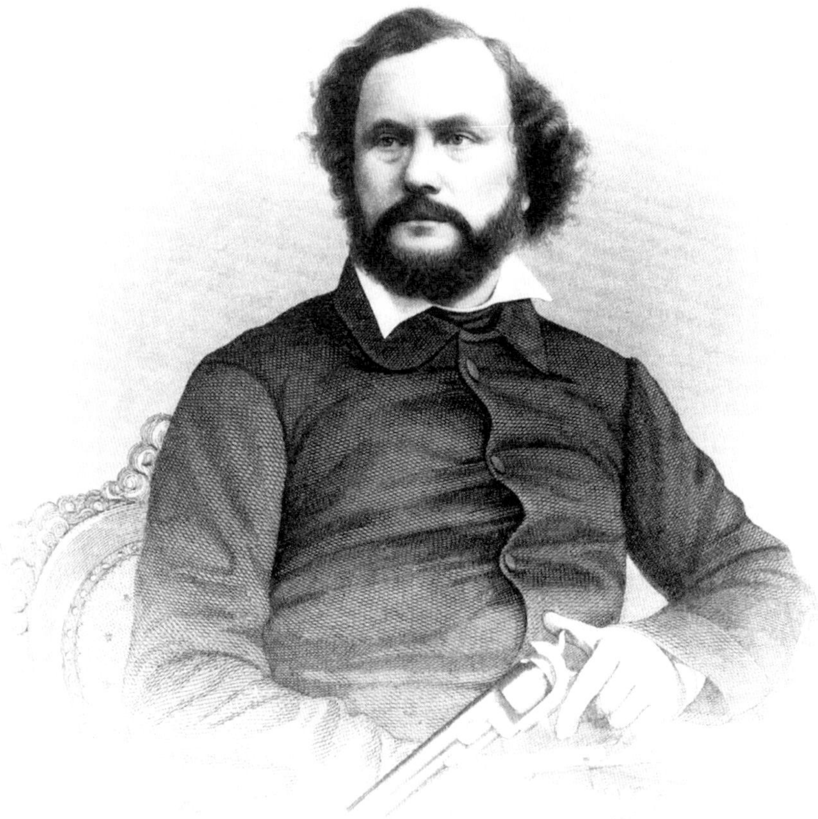

Samuel Colt, the "revolving patriot." *Engraving based on daguerreotype by Philipp Graff, approximately 1847.*

of bribing congressmen in 1854, Colt was back in Washington, D.C., the next year to buy votes for a patent extension. He promised he was "willing to pay handsome contingent fees [and] bend myself to pay in all $50,000… when the patent extension has become law." Today, that $50,000 is worth about $1 million. Colt specified that it should be split equally between the two political parties.

Does being an army officer make one a good businessman? Not in Colt's case: he was a terrible military man. He started to build a personal army (under his sole command), a very undemocratic move. To keep Colt under control, Governor William A. Buckingham made him a colonel. Colt told his recruits that once they signed up, they had to stay in his army for five years—far longer than the real U.S. Army requirement. He insisted that all his soldiers had to be at least five feet, seven inches tall, a height he simply made up. This excluded many qualified men, including some irate firemen from New Haven. Colonel Colt never saw battle. He was quickly stripped of his military command.

IMPERIAL LAND GRABS

Sam Colt also suffered from what might be called imperial overreach. He began with his quest to rule with "Coltsville," a company town within Hartford controlled by him from the bottom up. It had a library and other amenities, but that did no good to a worker who was arbitrarily fired and evicted from the company housing.

When his thirst for power increased, he bought an entire town. In June 1861, Colt purchased Lama, Texas, which was slave territory during the Civil War.

Colt's biggest land grab was international in scope. Colt historians note that the millionaire gun maker and some southern politicians aided Narcisco Lopez, a soldier of fortune who invaded Cuba twice, in 1850 and 1851, to "liberate" it, possibly so it could become a slave state. In any case, it would be a fine new market for Colt's weapons trade.

COLT'S WORKERS

The young, unmarried women who worked for him were employed to produce ammunition. These dangerous jobs were kept a safe distance from his precious weapons factory in case of an accidental explosion. For this extremely risky undertaking, the women were paid a fraction of what Colt's male employees earned.

It was Samuel Colt's position on slavery and abolition, the primary moral question of the day, that became his most shameful legacy. His defenders say Colt actually opposed slavery, citing a vague reference to a speaker who lectured his workers on the subject. The facts, however, tell a different story.

Colt decried the antislavery Republicans of the city and asked a political friend to publicly encourage manufacturers to fire employees who supported abolition. Northern business interests "promoted, prolonged and profited from slavery," according to *Complicity*, a book by three *Hartford Courant* reporters who documented the North's dependence on slavery to build financial empires.

His contemporaries accused him of voter suppression. Colt fired "black devil Republicans" (his words for antislavery partisans) from his factory. Colt even kept a secret journal on their political affiliations and fired workers whose politics strayed from his.

Colt's manipulation of his workforce was exposed at an 1860 meeting of Republican mechanics and workmen who had been discharged from Colt's factory. They met on March 20, five days after the firings and two weeks before the April presidential election. The men protested the terminations and declared, "the oppression of free labor by capital, and the attempt to coerce and control the votes of free men is an outrage upon the rights of the laboring classes."

The workers knew that of the sixty-six layoffs just ordered by Colt, fifty-six were active Republicans. This was a clear "tyrannical exertion of money-power," they asserted. The action forced those Republican voters out of town to look for work and created a chilling effect throughout the rest of Colt's workforce.

The angry men testified that Colt had previously required them to lobby city council meetings for a proposed bridge across the Connecticut River. The structure would allow Colt employees living in East Hartford easier access to their workplace, at the city's expense. Every worker understood that his "bread depended on his acquiescence" to the lobby effort.

In another example of political coercion, the Republicans uncovered the activities of Colt supervisor J. Deane Alden. His job was to stand by the ballot box and watch how each worker voted in the April 1859 aldermanic election. (Secret ballots were not the standard practice.) Colt's favored candidate, William W. Eaton, was elected, which tipped the balance of power on the board of aldermen. Eaton went on to become a U.S. senator.

Colt's operatives also employed a method dubbed the "Seymour books," so called after Thomas H. Seymour, the Democratic politician who was running for governor. These loyalty ledgers were circulated among the workforce. Men who did not sign were discharged.

Sam Colt insisted that the layoffs were the result of the company's overstock of weapons. Production had to be cut back, he explained. The explanation was highly implausible. In fact, his storehouse was so low that when a recent order came in, Colt had to "borrow" guns from the state arsenal to fill the demand.

The Republican workmen made a public plea to condemn Colt. Just because they were "under the necessity of laboring with our hands for our daily bread [this was] no reason why we may not have principles of our own." Certainly, their votes were as important as those of the plutocrats like Colt who "count their wealth by millions."

CONSORTING WITH THE ENEMY

Despite protests by his apologists, Sam Colt was a "copperhead," a Northern Democrat who opposed Lincoln and grew wealthy by arming traitors.

This profit connection was made crystal clear on December 16, 1859, at the Hartford city hall. The building was packed with local supporters of "states' rights," a coded phrase that justified Southern slavery.

Samuel Colt was one of the principal sponsors, listed as a "vice president" of the mass meeting. Colt joined the unanimous vote to condemn the abolitionists who were pressuring the South to end slavery.

Southern states were being unjustly attacked by "a class of men at the North who constantly harp at Slavery," charged one speaker. Another used thinly disguised racist rhetoric to make his point. "Lovers of negroes become haters of white men," former Hartford mayor William J. Hamersley told the crowd.

William W. Eaton connected the dots when he addressed the crowd of politicians and businessmen. "Look to your pockets," he told them. "We desire Southern cotton and corn. She is agricultural. She comes to us for her loans, insurance and goods. She is our best customer; and I have yet to learn that a sane business man will kick his best customer out of doors." Colt approved; he charged the U.S. Army 10 percent more than he charged the Confederate states for his weapons.

In January 1861, the *New York Times* issued a forceful criticism of Colt:

> *It is generally understood that COLT's establishment, and all the other manufactories of arms in Connecticut, are incessantly occupied—and have orders that it will take six months to fulfill—in making arms for the Southern States. It is perfectly understood, at the same time, that these arms*

> *are to be used in waging war against the United States. There is no attempt on any side to conceal this intention....*
>
> *Are the people of Connecticut content that the weapons for overthrowing the Government shall thus be furnished by their State?...Is it too much to expect that individuals should forego any chance of pecuniary profit which the calamities of their country may offer?*
>
> *Experience shows that with very many—perhaps with none more frequently than the rich and avaricious—all considerations of patriotism and the public good vanish in the presence of their selfish advantage.*

The Colonel sent his last shipment of guns to the South on April 15, 1861, three days *after* Fort Sumter was fired upon by Confederates. Word of the Charleston attack had traveled fast: Colt could read about it in the *Courant* one day after the assault. In addition, for an entire month prior to the attack, the newspapers were printing dispatches that detailed Southern troop movement and belligerent actions toward the South Carolina fort. Colt knew the war was coming, but he just didn't care.

Ten days before the Fort Sumter attack, U.S. District Court judge Peleg Sprague defined treason to a grand jury. His words were reprinted in the *Courant* on April 2, 1861. Sprague said: "A person, in league with those who were levying war, who should send them money, provisions, arms, or intelligence, for the purpose of aiding them was a traitor, no matter how far distant from them he might be."

On April 25, Colt offered to raise a regiment of able-bodied troops for the Northern war effort, thus earning the title of "revolving patriot." Governor Buckingham accepted the offer. All was forgiven.

Treason was already a federal crime in full force while Colt was packing up his guns for the South. Colt's actions clearly came under the provision of "giving aid and comfort" to the South. Likewise, Article 9 of the Connecticut Constitution defined treason as a crime. On June 19, the state's general assembly urged "the continued prosecution of a policy so *vigorous* and *resistless* that it will crush out treason now and forever."

COLT'S CRITICS

Some years after Colt's death, Mark Twain had a sardonic perspective about how arms manufacturing "closed the circle" between life and death in Hartford: "A city whose fame as an insurance center has extended to all lands and given us the name of being a quadruple band of brothers working sweetly hand in hand—the Colt's Arms Company making the destruction of our race easy and convenient, our life insurance citizens paying for the victims when they pass away, Mr. Batterson perpetuating their memory with his stately monuments, and our fire insurance companies taking care of their hereafter."

Eight years later, another article appeared in the *Courant* with the same theme. It was unsigned, but it is written in Twain's unmistakable style:

> *One becomes almost astonished at the importance of Connecticut in this line of business. We are the very headquarters of the killing industry. Look over the list.*
>
> *There is the Colt Company of this city, with its own revolving pistols and rifles, it's breech-loading shotguns and the famous Gatling gun as part of its projects. In the same city are the Pratt & Whitney works...manufacturing fine machinery for gun making, and also as the owners of the Gardner gun.*
>
> *Give us a murder or suicide and it but small chance that Connecticut didn't have a hand in it either with its powder, its cartridge, its revolver or its edge tool; and give us a war and we can furnish the material for any amount of slaughter.*
>
> *The fact is we make guns, and load them, and mean business.*

THE BIGAMIST AND THE MURDERER

Certainly, the most bizarre story surrounding Sam Colt concerns his brother, Hartford-born John Caldwell Colt, who was living in New York. John was angered by another businessman in 1841 and hacked the poor fellow to death. John chopped him up, stuffed him in a barrel and covered him with salt (to slow the decomposition). He then mailed the barrel to a fake address in New Orleans. The ploy might have worked, if the stink of the rotting corpse had not leaked through the barrel.

Brother Sam bought his brother the best legal defense available, but the jury still found him guilty. John was sentenced to hang.

On the morning of his execution, two astounding incidents took place. First, Sam had John marry young Caroline Henshaw in a jail-cell wedding. And just before his execution, John committed suicide with a knife smuggled

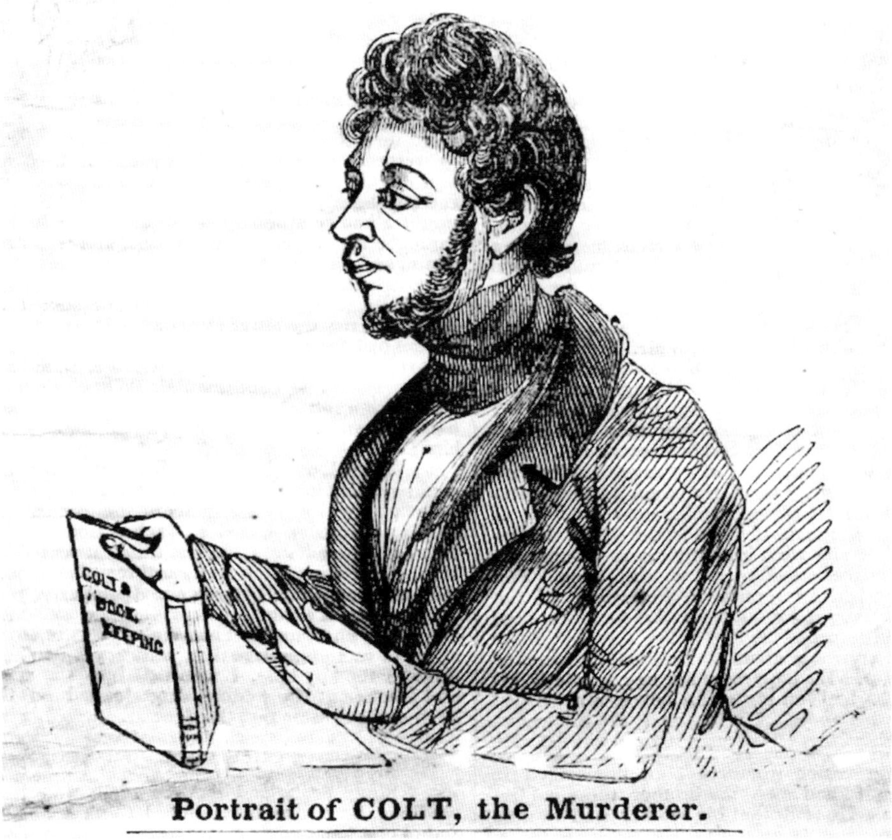

Sam's brother John C. Colt on trial. *Illustration by James E. Gourley. 1832. Digital Public Library of America.*

in past the guards. It was never established whether the guards had been bribed. No one knows who brought him the knife.

Caroline Henshaw's background was another source of scandal. Sam Colt had met the Scottish girl on a European trip. He wooed her and in 1838 married her in secret. He then moved her to New York. She produced a son and named him Sam. The Colonel was partial to the boy and described him in letters as his "nephew." (Sam used the quotation marks to describe young Sammy.)

There is no documentation to show Sam ever divorced Caroline, but in 1856, he married Elizabeth Jarvis. Sammy later produced a marriage certificate between Sam and Caroline that helped him gain access to the Colt fortune.

UNSUNG HEROES

Given this unseemly, immoral and criminal behavior, some have argued Colt really doesn't deserve all the positive attention he has received. There are certainly others who better qualify as local heroes in Hartford history. One contemporary of Samuel Colt was the Reverend James Pennington, a Hartford minister who was actually a fugitive slave. Pennington risked his life to escape to freedom, then risked it over and over again by advocating abolition from his Talcott Street pulpit. Not a penny of public funds has ever been spent to honor Pennington.

THE SPANISH GOUT

Most mysterious of all is the delicate subject of Sam Colt's death in 1862. Depending on the accounts, the cause of Colt's death was either rheumatic fever (serious if not treated, but not fatal), stress from overwork (although he and his family vacationed in Martha's Vineyard, Maryland, Havana and Europe), gout (chronic but not fatal) or gout plus a slight cold that "went to his brain." The only type of "gout" that goes to the brain is Spanish gout, a euphemism for syphilis. In a 2007 interview, however, one Colt historian firmly stated that the syphilis rumor "is almost certainly not true."

A QUESTIONABLE LEGACY

Some people are pretty desperate for heroes. What other explanation could there be for the attempts to glorify this merchant of death? His nineteenth-century factory has been established as a National Historic Landmark, even though Sam Colt never stepped foot inside. The original, built by Colt, burned to the ground four years after his death in 1864.

His widow, Elizabeth, built another in its place and promptly started production of Gatling guns, the first weapon of mass destruction—it could shoot five hundred rounds a minute. She constructed the Church of the Good Shepherd in honor of her dead husband. It included a bizarre stained-glass window featuring Sam as the biblical figure Joseph from the Old Testament. Atop the "armorer's arch" entrance, Christian crosses

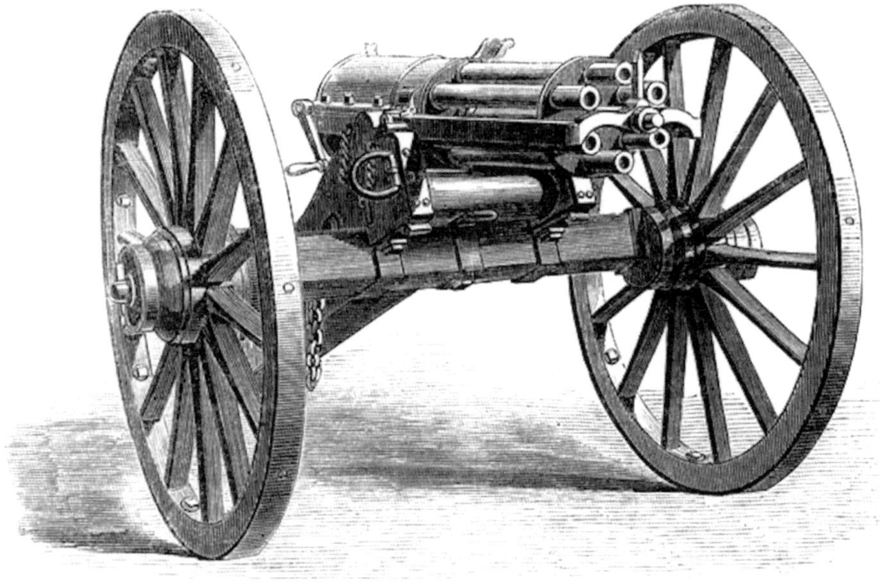

Made in Hartford: Dr. Gatling's weapon of mass destruction. *From American Civil War Stories.com.*

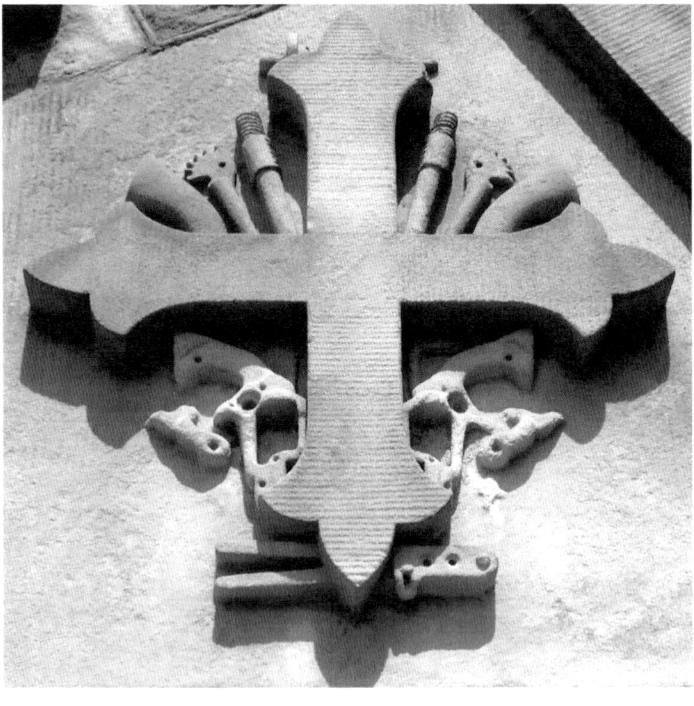

Decoration on Colt's Church of the Good Shepherd at the east entrance "Armorer's Porch." Note the gun parts around the intersection of the cross. These areas of a crucifix usually denote the divinity of Jesus. *Author's photo.*

were decorated with parts of Colt handguns. Elizabeth became a patron of the arts, but charity does not excuse the sins of the Colt family.

Sam Colt supporters can put up as many memorials to the Colonel as they want. Colt gets high marks for being a wealthy businessman and a great self-promoter. But his story reads like the worst excesses in the first chapter of the Gilded Age.

3
HOBOES, TRAMPS AND BUMS

The homeless workers who rode freight trains and knocked on Hartford doors for handouts have always been caricatured in fiction and in the press. They were considered a nuisance at best, at worst a danger to the community. Hartford sheltered them, shunned them, legislated against them and tried to reform the itinerant men (and sometimes women) who otherwise clogged the city's jail cells. But even the experimental efforts of Trinity College's Reverend John James McCook could not get at the source of the "tramp problem."

One evening as the sun went down
And the jungle fires were burning,
Down the track came a hobo hiking,
And he said, Boys, I'm not turning
I'm headed for a land that's far away
Besides the crystal fountains
So come with me, we'll go and see
The Big Rock Candy Mountains

In the Big Rock Candy Mountains
All the cops have wooden legs
The bulldogs all have rubber teeth
And the hens lay soft-boiled eggs
The farmers' trees are full of fruit
And the barns are full of hay

In the Big Rock Candy Mountains,
The jails are made of tin
And you can walk right out again
As soon as you are in
There ain't no short-handled shovels
No axes, saws or picks
I'm gonna to stay
Where you sleep all day,
Where they hung the jerk
That invented work
In the Big Rock Candy Mountains.

This original hobo's version of the children's song contrasts sharply with the reality of being a tramp in Hartford throughout the late nineteenth and early twentieth centuries. Examples of the hobo's life can still be found in the North Meadows at the edge of Hartford's railroad yard.

Originally, most tramps had been tradesmen or artisans: weavers, shoemakers, machinists, masons. They were workers who could not find jobs in the financial crash of the 1870s, and their numbers increased as one economic slump followed another right up to the Great Depression of the 1930s. "The financial troubles of the past few years have done a great deal to spread pauperism through the country by their indirect as well as their direct influence," observed one Hartford writer.

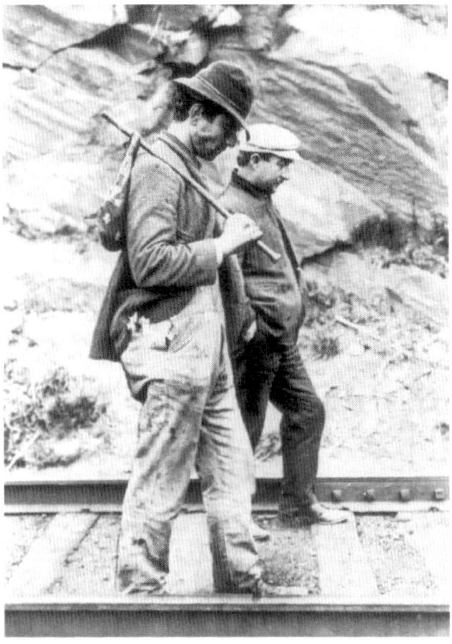

Hoboes have tramped through Hartford since the 1800s. *Library of Congress.*

The problem has not disappeared. Louise Newkirk, for many years in the 1970s a cook in a local Hartford daycare center, recalled as a child the tar-paper shack hobo jungle populated by men and women who had been discarded by—or who had rejected—proper society.

Many hoboes rode the rails, building a culture of language and ethics that still exists today. Hopping the freights with the unemployed were the Wobblies—labor organizers for the Industrial Workers of the World (IWW), the "One Big Union" that rocked the textile industry in Lawrence, Massachusetts; organized workers in Hartford; and spread the union cause throughout the country. Hoboes and Wobblies had a common antagonist in the Pinkerton Agency, a private police army that operated in Hartford and around the nation. It specialized in busting unions and breaking heads in factories and railroad yards. Allan Pinkerton's account of his exploits was set down in his book *Strikers, Communists, Tramps and Detectives.*

HOBOES AS CRIMINALS AND ROMANTIC FIGURES

"Vagabonds, tramps and thieves" were banned from entering Hartford as far back as 1678, and Connecticut passed an anti-hobo law 1879. It defined tramps as "transient persons who rove about from place to place begging, and all vagrants living without labor, or visible means of support, who stroll over the country without lawful occasion." The penalty was up to one year in prison. The legislation, which did not cover minors, women and blind people, was eliminated in 1969.

During one month in 1871, police counted a total of 779 "tramps and destitute people" lodged at the station house on Kinsley Street. Some whole families applied for shelter. Newspapers of the day printed stories variously designating hoboes as "religious tramps," "insolent tramps," "aggressive tramps" and "suspicious tramps."

The Connecticut legislature passed its anti-tramp law in March 1879. Opponents of the bill pointed to economic hardships and violation of Christian principles. By law, every town was given the legal right to make an unemployed man work. "His refusal alone constitutes an offense punishable by imprisonment for not less than thirty days nor more than six months," wrote a local newspaper. "It is under this law that the compulsory measures have been applied in Hartford." The law was not consistently enforced, although it did add to another type of danger for men who tramped the roads.

Tramps and hoboes had few advocates, but occasionally they were able to speak for themselves. Here is one Hartford man who reacted to the constant public drumbeat against tramps:

> *I am a tramp. I do not take papers, but I understand that you newspaper men pitch into us pretty often, and I hope you will allow a word from our side.*

> *Let me tell, in brief, my own story. I am thirty years old, an unmarried man, with none for me to depend on. I was born in a country town of Massachusetts. At eight years old I was an orphan and destitute. I worked my way along as I could, picked up a trade and a tolerable common school education, and notwithstanding some head flaws, paid my way and laid up a little, till last winter; working for the last four years in a machine shop in South Boston.*
>
> *Then I had a long sickness from lung fever, and at the end was pretty well stripped, for doctors and nurses and boarding house keepers, you know, must have something to eat as well as tramps, and are not bashful in asking for it. Getting out again, I repaired at once to the machine shop, but behold! it had shut down. No more chance for me there. I went round and round to other shops. No, was the constant answer. "More men than we want already."*
>
> *I went down upon the wharves. The longshoremen were loafing and playing cards, waiting for something to do. Vessel after vessel was stripped and idle. No chance for me there. I went among the farmers. "No, no" was the answer; "we have hands enough."* [In Hartford] *these four weeks I have had just three days work, two from a farmer, and one from a country minister.*
>
> *Here I am now. Look at me. You say I am ragged and dirty. Very likely, the former results from the fact that clothes will wear out, especially if they are a cheat to begin with, and the latter from the fact that I have lodged for weeks in your Connecticut town houses....I am a born Yankee, intelligent, tough, wiry, willing to work, but no chance.*
>
> *Do I deserve to be scouted and spit upon, and to have the dogs set on me because I go from town to town, begging for work, or, in default of that, for a crust of bread to keep me alive?*
>
> *Yes, Mr. Editor, I am that hateful thing, a tramp. And let me tell you there are multitudes just like me.*

The editor responded that "for everyone honest unfortunate sufferer, there are fifty frauds who beg because it is easier than to work." He called the increase in unemployed men who could not find work "the tramp industry."

Not every attitude toward hoboes was unsympathetic. In the early twentieth century, Hartford's Socialist Labor Party campaigned to eliminate "tramp laws" used to jail the homeless. Hartford residents in the 1890s read tales like "John Smith, Tramp," a short story about a mysterious stranger who approaches a widow for help. "Are you brute or human?" she demands as she points a gun at him. The woman eventually allows the ragged man to work for room and board, but he soon quietly disappears. A few months later, he sends the widow a check for her kindness. She discovers he is a judge who took to the roads after mistakenly believing he had killed his wife.

REVEREND JOHN AND ROVING BILL

The study of hoboes was often relegated to such romantic folklore. But Trinity College professor and clergyman John McCook made it his business to study the lives of displaced people from 1890 until his death in 1927. McCook surveyed, photographed and corresponded with men like Pittsburgh Phil and Connecticut Fatty to get to the root of the "tramp problem," which he initially ascribed to personal defects. He focused on the use of hoboes by local politicians for what was called "venal voting," or vote buying. He even set up a citizens' committee, which he said included Pinkerton agents, to monitor polling places.

McCook also proposed government control and distribution of liquor and the establishment of a reformatory where vagrants would work for their room and board. Attempting to have the state institution built on Fairfield Avenue, McCook seriously misjudged the political opposition of wealthy neighbors; the plan was abandoned after years of work.

It was William Wesley "Roving Bill" Aspinwall who tried to show Dr. McCook that the clergyman's solutions were superficial. Bill and McCook corresponded for almost twenty-five years. Bill wrote to McCook (with paper and postcards provided by the preacher) on the road from Niagara Falls to Mexico. Bill traveled to Europe and around the world, stopping in Calcutta, Bombay, Australia and the West Indies. He had originally been a worker at a Rhode Island woolen mill. On the road, Bill was a "mush faker," that is, a man who repaired umbrellas. One photo of him reveals the tools of his trade: a wooden box with a shoulder strap, along with canes and umbrella sticks.

Bill taught McCook many things, not the least of which was what type of men made up the hobo community. He wrote (with his own spelling and turns of phrase):

> *There is several clases of tramps or Haut Beaus. I can make about three out of them with occasionally a woman. There is 1st the Harmless Tramp*

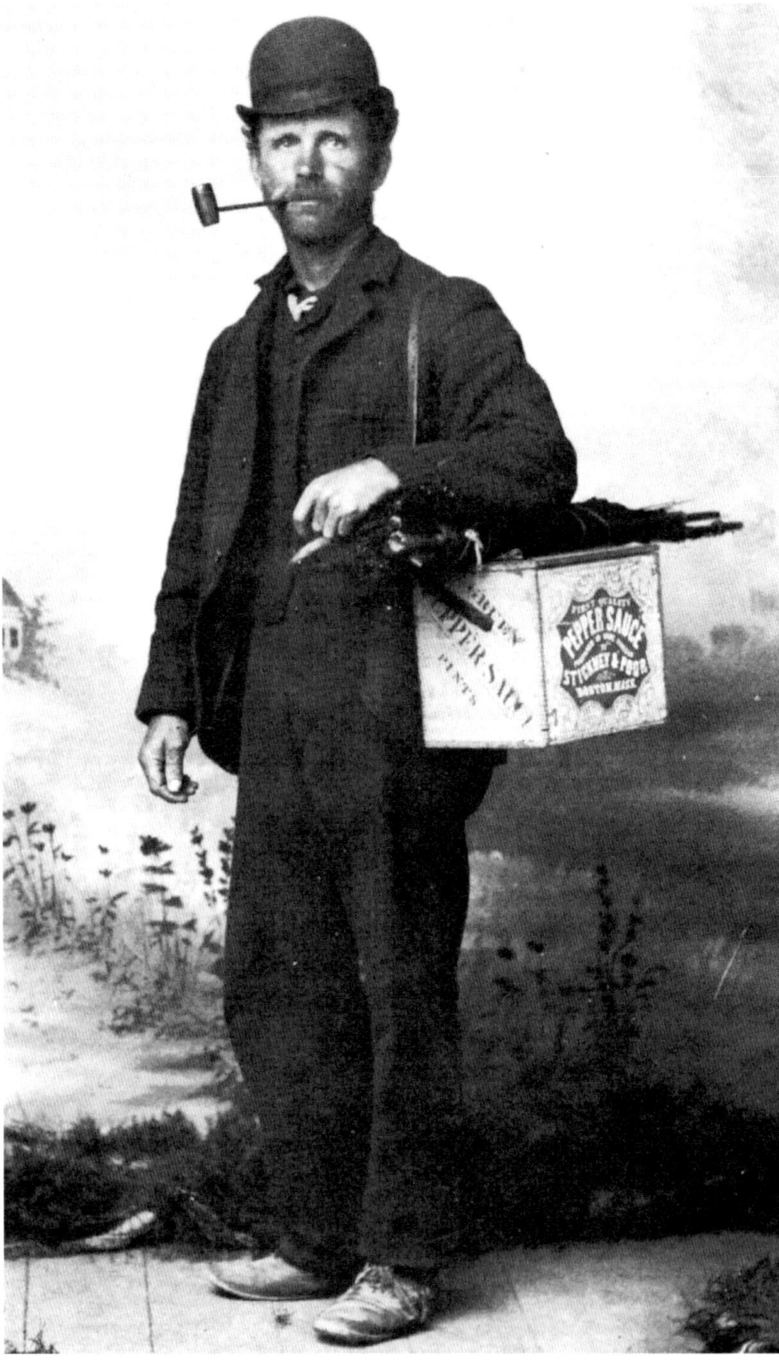

Roving Bill Aspinwall, the hobo who taught the Reverend Dr. John James McCook a few things. Independent *53, no. 2764, November 21, 1901.*

that tramps because he has no home. No Friends and got on the road from Drink and then No. 2 is Fakers and Mush Fakers, Mechanics and others on the Tramp hunting network, and some of the finest mechanics in the country, comprising all trades, get on the road by spending their money too liberal and Partly from drink and get down and ashamed to ask for a Job, and good fellows there are, will divide the last nickel with you or the last Biscuit.

There appears to be a kind of Brotherly feeling amongst this Class, but they have no use for Class No. 3 as they are composed of ex Convicts, Jail Birds and Regular Dead Beats. There is some mean Haut Beaus that will venture to do anything—insult Women, steal and fire barns, Can't be trusted. This makes it bad for an Honest man as the Public thinks they are all Chips of the same block, but far from it. Just as much difference in the Classes as there is in the Classes of societies in a Citty, or a Vilage.

ALCOHOL: CAUSE OR EFFECT?

Aspinwall, a Civil War veteran who had suffered a head injury, was frank about his drinking problem. But unlike McCook, he considered it more the result of his inability to stay employed, not the other way around. His travels allowed him to become a barometer of the country's financial condition; the more tramps he met on the road, the more he recognized another depression was coming.

Like many others, Bill was a victim of capitalism's boom-and-bust cycle. He believed that if Dr. McCook wanted to rid Hartford of vice and alcohol abuse, the solution was full employment. As he wrote to McCook, society had to "abolish industrial booms, financial crises, business slumps, hard times!"

Hobo life rose with the railroads and the chaos created by the race for profits. Hartford's hobo neighborhood was bulldozed to make way for Interstate Route 91. Nowadays, homeless shelters have largely replaced fleabag hotels and hobo jungles in the city. But when hard times hit, the unemployed and homeless seek out more independent ways to live.

Today, you will still find individuals or small tribes of homeless men and women spending their summers in an abandoned trailer truck near the north Hartford railroad tracks or under the giant highway bridges.

4
THE SCOURGE OF ALCOHOL

At the dawn of the twentieth century, more than 180 saloons crowded Hartford streets—two dozen on Front Street alone. They were stocked by local breweries. There were twice as many bars as all the local churches and temperance groups combined.

Many of Hartford's immigrant families considered wine a part of their diets and culture. For many adults, booze was a harmless recreational activity; for some, a deadly addiction. For still others, alcohol was a source of employment and a signifier of community, as well.

Four breweries served the bars and taverns of Hartford: Hubert Fischer, New England Brewing, Aetna Brewing and Ropkins & Company. They produced four hundred barrels of beer each week, 75 percent of all the alcohol consumed in the city.

In April 1902, Hartford brewery workers went on strike. They labored sixty-two hours a week for less than ten dollars and were demanding an eight-hour day. Local 36 of the Brewers' Union went to bars all over the city to make sure owners were not buying "scab" beer, even though the four breweries were completely shut down.

They also went to other unions and asked them to pledge not to drink beer until the strike was settled. For the hardworking, hard-drinking members of Hartford's working class, this was a significant act of solidarity.

The beer makers, who were mostly German immigrants, had significant support in their fight. The local building trades, clerks and metalworkers' unions offered moral and financial aid. Louis Eisel, John Doyle and Matthew

Kelly of the Hartford Central Labor Union headed the negotiations with the owners. Most significant, there was a "non-interference" agreement from union breweries all over the country that in the case of a strike, no additional beer would be shipped into the city.

The strike was cause for a re-examination by Hartford workers of their commitment to unionism and particularly to union-made goods. According to news reports, men checked each other's suits for union labels and chastised those who smoked non-union tobacco.

Going without their daily staple was a true sacrifice for fellow workers. Some sympathizers even began to drink ginger ale in place of beer.

Within six days (including one Saturday night), the strike was over and the workers had won. Bartenders' Union leaders J.J. Murphy and T.J. Sullivan got involved and spoke to both the strikers and the owners. The result was impressive by any standard: the Brewers' Union won the eight-hour day and more control over their jobs.

And the brewery workers won five minutes off each hour to drink beer.

PROMISING ATHLETE, TRAGIC CASUALTY: LOUIS SOCKALEXIS

It is unlikely in 1900 that there was anyone in Hartford who did not know the name Louis Francis Sockalexis. A Penobscot Indian born in Old Town, Maine, he demonstrated extraordinary athletic ability as a teenager and played a variety of sports at Holy Cross College and Notre Dame.

Baseball was his game, and he was recruited to the National League's Cleveland Spiders in 1897. Sockalexis played with greats like Cy Young and hit .338 in his first sixty games, causing hall of famer John McGraw to call him the greatest natural talent he had ever seen. Sockalexis spent two full seasons in the big leagues with Cleveland.

Separated from his island reservation, his tribe and the forests of Maine, he became an early victim of hard drinking and fast living and was a target of frequent hostility and racism from crowds and players. On road trips through Baltimore, Brooklyn and Boston, Sockalexis endured bigoted insults beyond the normal taunting his teammates received. He responded to racial prejudice with great dignity.

Early in the 1899 season, Sockalexis was released from pro baseball after his performance suffered, due in part to an alcohol-related injury.

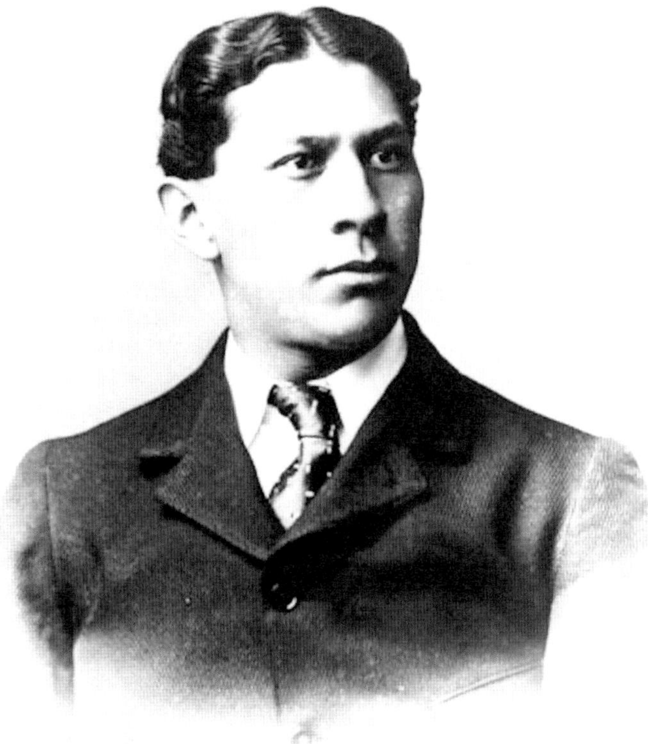

Louis Sockalexis, first Native American professional baseball player. *The Baseball Reliquary.*

He was immediately picked up by the semi-pro Hartford Chiefs while the team was in New York playing the Rochester Broncos. Sockalexis had to put up with the stereotyping of his race while in Hartford, especially from some very bad "Hiawatha" parodies by local sportswriters.

The young Penobscot had not beaten his alcohol addiction when he moved to Hartford. Although he had promised his manager that he would reform, the temptation was all around him. By June, published stories circulated that "Sox" was "working the night-owl racket."

His last local news account revealed that Sockalexis had "kept bad hours and as a result when he went after a ball his movements reminded one of a messenger boy on an errand."

After Hartford, he took another step down, this time to the Connecticut State League. Recruited by a team in Bristol, Sockalexis was quickly stolen away by Roger Connors's Waterbury club, where he successfully finished out the season and helped the team reach second place. It was the one season when his drinking seemed to be under control.

By next spring, it was reported that Louis Sockalexis was back in Hartford, a vagrant who frequented Front Street taverns. His biographer Brian McDonald says he worked for a time in some capacity at Colt Firearms.

He moved closer and closer to home, first to Massachusetts, then to Maine, still involved with baseball as a player, an umpire or as a coach for aspiring young Penobscot ballplayers. Louis Sockalexis died in 1913 on Christmas Eve while working as a logger in the forest near his home.

PROHIBITION GETS A LUKEWARM RECEPTION

Prohibition was a grassroots effort that succeeded in 1919 with the passage of the Eighteenth Amendment to the Constitution, otherwise known as the Volstead Act. In the years before the law was passed, temperance and prohibition meetings crowded Allyn Hall and churches across Hartford.

Connecticut, however, was one of the two states that never ratified the federal law. Rhode Island was the other. The Connecticut General Assembly did, however, pass its own liquor ban in 1921, imposing $2,000 fines and two years in prison for selling or transporting alcohol for any reason except medical use.

Until the passage of Prohibition, Connecticut cities and towns could choose whether or not to allow the sale of liquor within their boundaries. Hartford and seventy-five other towns were "wet," and ninety-one were "dry." In all the big cities, and for the majority of the state's population, alcohol was legal.

The Volstead Act was unpopular in Hartford and widely ignored. A state report from the Wickersham Commission determined that arrests actually rose from 1920 to 1929 for the violation of liquor laws and intoxication in Hartford and the state's four other big cities.

In fact, there were only thirteen federal agents assigned to Connecticut for enforcement of the liquor ban. Two of them were arrested by the state police in 1924 for running a massive liquor smuggling ring.

Hugh Alcorn, the state attorney for Hartford County, burnished his public image when he waged an "aggressive war" on liquor distribution. He focused police raids on the city's poor, predominantly Italian east side. No corresponding assaults, apparently, were undertaken where Hartford's rich and famous wined and dined.

MARIJUANA AND OPIUM

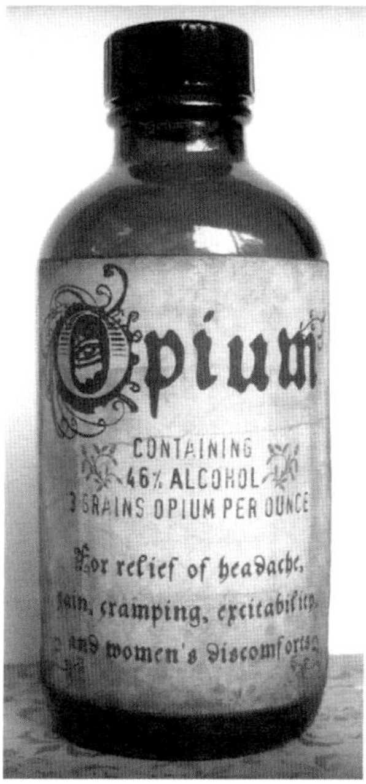

Opium, sold in drug dens and pharmacies. *Yesteryear News*.

"Marihuana is a weed used by people of the lower class and sometimes by soldiers," declared the *Hartford Courant* in 1907. Just three or four puffs would "make the smoker wilder than the wild beast." The result of marijuana use caused "people who smoke marihuana [to] finally lose their mind, and never recover it, but their brains dry up and they die, most of times suddenly."

While marijuana's image was ugly, the smoking of opium was another story. At the start of the twentieth century, it was not illegal to sell or smoke the drug. In fact, interested Hartford readers learned that in 1909 a British commission had just pronounced opium smoking "relatively harmless."

At the time, China was attempting to halt the opium epidemic among its population. The major hurdle came from Great Britain: its colony of India was a major opium producer, and China was an important market. British gunboats kept the trade lines open, from Asia to Hartford, even provoking the "Opium Wars" against China to keep England's East India Company in business. Yes, the same early corporation that supplied taxed tea to the American colonies in 1773 also held the monopoly on Indian opium.

For only one dollar, any Hartford resident could purchase a "toy of hop" for a single smoke. An investigative newspaper report in 1907 described in great detail the process of cooking the drug. The description was almost romantic: the drug gave off a "warm spice odor"; the substance turned "golden brown" when cooked. According to the article, there were as many as four hundred opium smokers in Hartford at the time.

The largest den was on State Street, in the basement of Yeung Sing & Company, a tea and spice dealer. For more than a decade, Mr. Sing had been the city's highest-profile Chinese resident. In 1914, one hundred pounds of crude opium were confiscated by local authorities. The next year, Yeung Sing's place was raided; Hartford police found $30,000 (in today's dollars) of the stuff.

Opium from Turkey was imported to Hartford as early as 1840 by the Lee & Butler business and sold at the Good Samaritans store on Main Street. (England also held a strategic interest in Turkey.) In its respectable form, opium-laced items could be found in Hartford drugstores.

The drug was becoming very popular, widely used in cordials and health elixirs. It was sold in the painkiller laudanum and in paregoric for upset stomachs. Most horrifying, opium was given to children to make them more manageable. "Infants were kept under the influence of the narcotic day and night, from week to week," one report revealed.

Congress banned the importation of opium in 1909, the first of many such substances made illegal, kicking off the "War on Drugs." It wasn't until 1923, two years after Prohibition, that all narcotics were made illegal.

5

BABY FARMING IN HARTFORD?

Baby farming was "the undertaker for the unwanted baby's death," wrote one social reformer just two years before a scandal rocked Hartford. City missionary Virginia Thrall Smith was accused of trafficking in children for private profit. It was an odious charge that she could never fully escape.

> *Baby farming was condemned for being lethal, profitable, and at odds with child welfare. At a time when public health reformers documented astronomical rates of infant mortality in poor, congested urban communities and congregate institutions, it came as no surprise that babies consigned to farms often died there, victims of epidemic disease and unsanitary conditions.*
>
> *The entrepreneurial side of baby farming was also used to vilify extreme forms of commercial adoption, in which babies were bought and sold like other commodities. Baby farmers sometimes profited on both ends of the adoption transaction, first extracting fees from desperate birth mothers and then demanding large sums from adopters.*

So writes Ellen Herman in the Adoption History Project. The phrase "baby farm" was, and will always be, a pejorative term. It was first used in Victorian England, where scandals of child abuse and death exploded on the front pages of British newspapers. The *Hartford Courant* was happy to revive the term and apply it to the 1892 charity efforts by Virginia Smith.

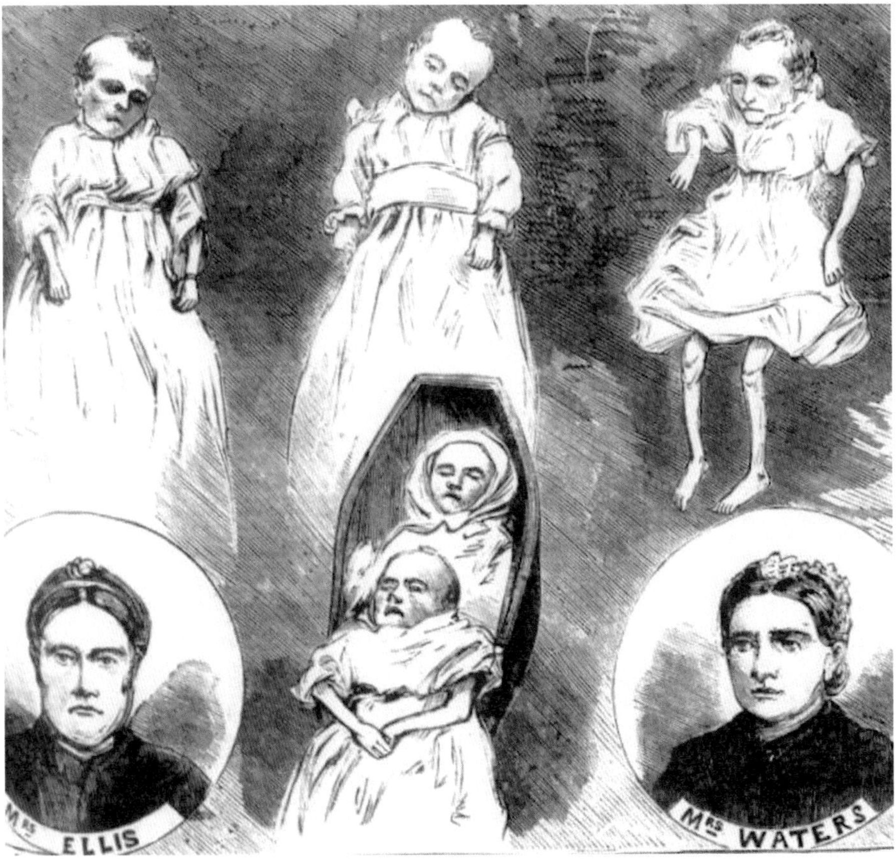

The "baby farming" panic began in Victorian England, as illustrated by this gruesome sketch. *Illustrated Police News, 1870.*

There was only one problem: the charges against Smith weren't true. Rather, they were fabricated by George W. Fowler, known for decades as Hartford's "shrewdest politician."

WAYWARD GIRLS

The baby farming phenomenon arose from a rise in illegitimate children. The stigma associated with having "loose morals" always fell on the woman, not the man who "betrayed" or "ruined" her. Virginia Smith rejected that notion because it inevitably led to the neglect of both the women and the children in need. The harder Smith worked, the greater her reputation grew for being the one person everyone could turn to. One example illustrated her renown:

> *Miss Nellie Louisa Abbott, who looks to be 17 and says she is 13, was taken from the Union depot early this morning and locked up in the women's ward. She had been at the depot for some time and wanted to go to Boston, but did not have any money. At the police station she said she had run away from the Children's Aid Society on Haynes Street. She said that Mr. Abbott of Boston, an electrician, was her adopted father and when he went to the Klondike some time ago he did not think his wife should take care of her so she came to this city. She said her own parents were supposed to be Mr. and Mrs. Graves of Pomfret and when she went to them they turned her out of the house. She was placed by Mrs. Virginia T. Smith with a Mrs. Way of New Britain.*

THE ACCUSATIONS

Smith's work rankled First Selectman George W. Fowler. His criticism centered on the placement of neglected children in "temporary homes" instead of keeping them in almshouses (which Fowler controlled). John Hooker, one of Smith's strongest supporters, exposed Fowler's "personal hostility" toward Smith, in part because she insisted the almshouse should be open to regular inspections. Virginia Smith and other advocates passed state legislation to this effect in 1888. From that time on, Fowler watched her activities "with an unfriendly eye."

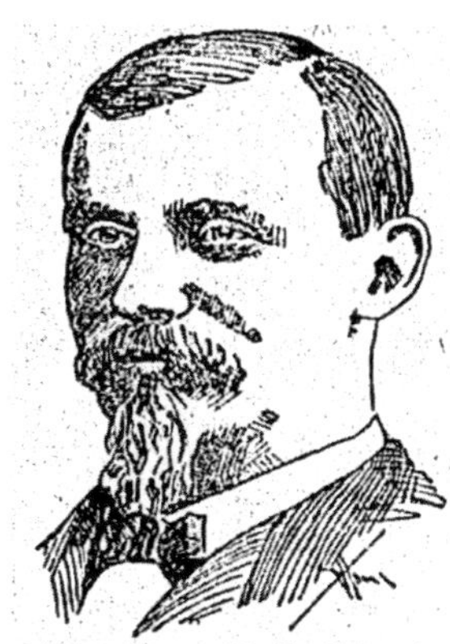

George Fowler, powerful Hartford alderman and Virginia T. Smith's nemesis. *Author's collection.*

The temporary care solution had the government place needy children from two to sixteen years of age until they could be adopted or placed with families we would now call foster parents. This prevented kids from being stuck in the Asylum Hill almshouse, to "save them from becoming paupers," wrote Hooker. "In the almshouse, boys became paupers, tramps or inmates." Girls suffered an even worse fate, he declared:

> *With the disgrace of growing up in an almshouse hanging over them, and the discredit, in so many cases attending their birth, they would never acquire that first essential of good character—self-respect, and would probably never be able to marry even respectably, and, in the great majority of cases, would repeat the maternal immorality and make illegitimacy a constant heritage through succeeding generations. In addition to this there would be a large result of pauperism, which would become a charge on the public, not to speak of a high-handed crime. Thus the moral and economic disadvantages of the almshouse system for such children can hardly be overstated.*

Hooker put the responsibility for the misery of the Hartford almshouse squarely on Fowler. Hooker predicted it was an "inevitable pit that his system has dug for him."

Hooker illustrated the severe neglect created by the poverty cycle with an infamous example of the period:

> *Margaret was a pauper child left adrift in one of the villages on the upper Hudson, nearly one hundred years ago. She became the mother of a long race of criminals and paupers which have cursed that part of the country ever since. The records of the county show 200 of her descendants who have been prosecuted as criminals, and many others were drunkards or prostitutes. The cost to the county was estimated...as at least $100,000, taking no account of damage done by them to property, and the suffering and degradation they caused to others.*

George Fowler issued his own report on August 5, 1892, in front of the Hartford selectmen. He did not use a frontal assault against the foster care option. Rather than attacking Virginia Smith's many accomplishments, he charged that she had not notified the selectmen of an adoption transaction, had demanded adoptive parents pay more than the actual costs for the service and had used her 39 Imlay Street home to house illegitimate children. Fowler also accused Smith of profiting from the "hush money" fathers gave her so the men would not be exposed. These practices were shrouded in secrecy, Fowler insisted.

Hooker demolished all the charges. It was not Virginia Smith's responsibility to inform the selectmen when children were placed, Hooker explained. There were no set adoption fees.

One woman who complained against Smith was angry that her child was illegitimate. "Had I known it I would not have taken it," Fowler's witness said. This same complainant also charged, without evidence, that she paid Smith personally for the child. The accusation, however, came four years after the adoption, and a credible witness testified that the accuser knew the child's status all the time.

Fowler held to the idea that proper care for illegitimate children encouraged "profligate men in vice." The day would never come, John Hooker countered, "though Mr. Fowler may shrink from contemplating it, when a baby left on a doorstep will not be taken in and cared for." For more than fifteen years, Hooker reminded the public, Smith had helped 1,200 Hartford children "on their way from wretchedness to comfort and hope."

Hooker also exposed Fowler's attempt to entrap Smith regarding a phony letter, allegedly from a widowed woman who wanted to adopt. The "widow" asked Smith for confidentiality, which Smith promised in writing. Fowler produced the letter and charged that Virginia Smith "induced" this woman to adopt, with a promise "to be shady about it." Fowler wrote (in a widely distributed pamphlet):

> *Is it conducive to public morality for fast young men to understand that a convenient place can be found where, for money, the girl they have betrayed can be put, where "the strictest secrecy is observed?" They* [the keepers of baby farms] *are told to ask no questions and to answer no questions... it is not an act of charity to assist young men and women to cover up their evil deeds, and thus to make easy the paths of immorality, and in these cases it is not in the interest of good morals.*

"Not a dollar has ever been taken by me, directly or indirectly, for any such service or purpose," responded Smith. Taking in young, unmarried pregnant women had never been "the means of a penny's profit to me." The male seducers, Smith noted, were the last people she would ever expect to hear from.

Fowler indicated there were hundreds of such cases; the record showed there were only eight cases in which unwed mothers were boarded.

He called the instances of care examples in which the child "could be quietly disposed of."

"Was the object...to find a home for a motherless baby in a Christian family, *or to get rid of a bastard?*" (emphasis Fowler's). He counted as "baby farms" area homes where the families actually provided competent and loving foster care.

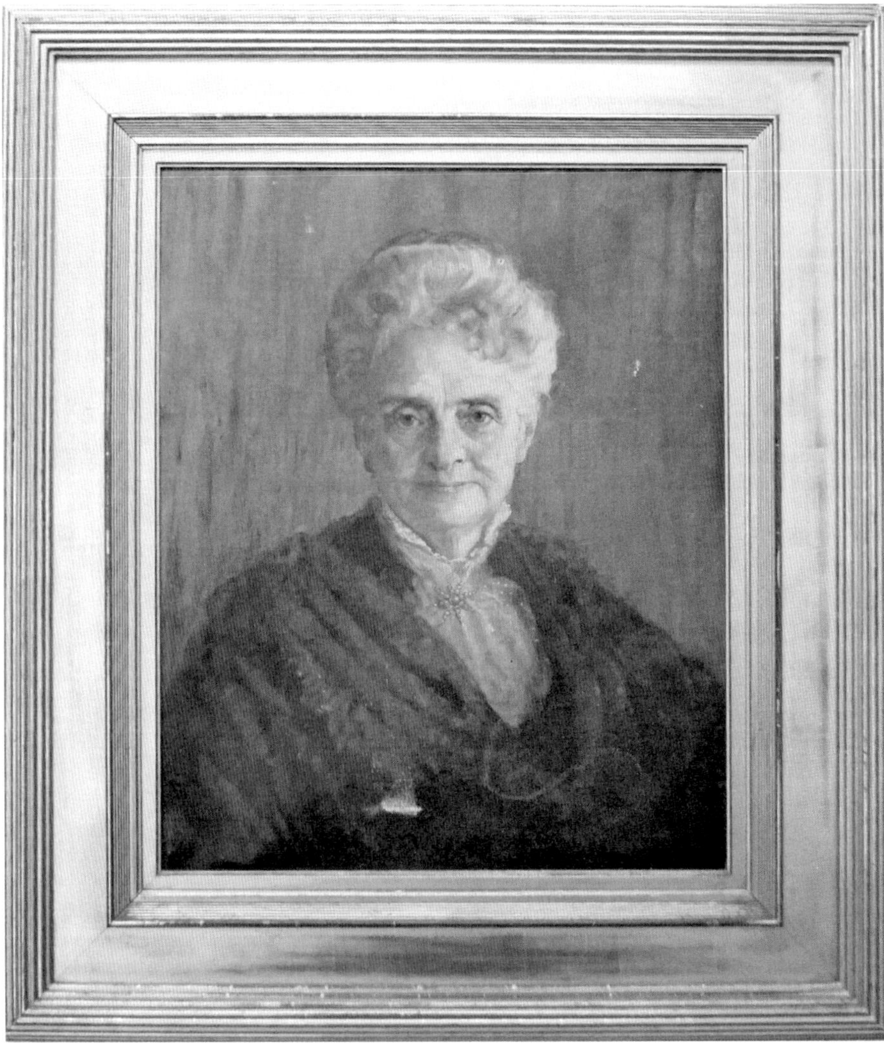

Virginia Thrall Smith. *Courtesy of the Butterworth family and the Village for Families and Children.*

Fowler offered no proof for these accusations. "I was unable to get sufficient evidence to justify official action," Fowler admitted.

Virginia Smith helped every young woman or child, black or white, in need. Most, if not all, of them were poor and had no family options. Often the affected children were physically disabled and required extraordinary care.

George Fowler could not even tell the truth about a meeting between himself and Dr. Oliver Cotton Smith, Virginia Smith's son. Fowler insisted that there was no bad blood between himself and Virginia. As evidence, he described a time when Dr. Smith visited his office simply to compliment Fowler's good work. Dr. Smith was flabbergasted. He publicly contradicted Fowler: the real purpose of their meeting was to ask Fowler's aid on a child's behalf and to criticize Fowler for his attacks on Virginia.

Finally, George Fowler suggested that someone had attempted to bribe a local newspaper so it would not print the unfavorable stories against Virginia. Again, he made the charge but provided no evidence.

Why would Fowler so adamantly oppose the inspection of Hartford's almshouse? One likely reason: patronage. The almshouse was a city creation. It was supplied by businesses that contracted with the city. Every contract was approved by George Fowler.

At one point, suppliers delivered to almshouse "inmates" cartons of whiskey and tobacco worth $62,000 a year (in today's dollars), billed to the city. The facility's overseer, Robert White, was dismissed because he was caught selling overpriced corned beef for the inhabitants. After White's termination, private firms including the Long Brothers were hired to prepare better meals for the almshouse. These contracts provided other opportunities to spread patronage around. Fowler ran Hartford like the political boss he was.

It was clear that he also hated the idea of a woman possessing the audacity to challenge his power. He wanted Virginia Smith to pay the price for overstepping the Victorian boundaries set for her and every other woman. Fowler was the self-proclaimed enforcer of gender roles. His reaction to illegitimate births was to condemn the mother and excuse the father. This fortified the unwritten rule that women must be virgins until marriage.

Finally, Fowler saw his role as the defender of class boundaries. Virginia Smith wanted poor children to gain some advantages early in life. Fowler was happy to keep them in the almshouse and then maybe place them in reform schools. During this period in Hartford, the Irish were the fastest-growing ethnic group, and Fowler must have figured that there were plenty of openings for domestic workers and railway diggers.

THE REAL VIRGINIA T. SMITH

It was Christmas Eve, 1883. The temperature had dropped to eighteen degrees below zero across Hartford. A new snowstorm made travel all but impossible.

Virginia Smith read a newspaper article that morning about how a woman with a contagious disease was being turned away from Hartford Hospital. "I determined to drive at once to the pest house—and if the patient were able, to remove her to the industrial building of the City Mission," she wrote. "I found no path broken to the place, and calling on the almshouse to inquire how to reach it, was informed that there was no one in it." Smith made sure the woman was properly cared for in the almshouse. After the incident, she wrote: "Yet while this case is now provided for, the great need of a proper place for such cases still remains. In our work similar cases frequently occur and we often ask ourselves what can be done for them? We feel sure that if it is properly and thoroughly brought before our citizens we may, before another Christmas, have a place provided for this class so sorely needing care and nursing, and at present so utterly unable to receive it."

VIRGINIA AND WILLIAM

Virginia could not always raise her family in comfortable wealth, despite her social status. In fact, her highly effective charity work was triggered by personal hardship.

She was born Tryphena Virginia on August 16, 1836, to Melissa and Hiram Thrall, a Bloomfield businessman and surveyor. They provided her with a good education; Virginia's charitable instincts were probably sharpened at the Hartford Female Seminary.

Virginia married William Brown Smith in 1857. At various times he owned a tailor shop, blacksmith forge, carriage works and grain business. A terrible gambler, he literally lost the family farm. His real love was horses, which he raised and raced. His most famous stallion was Thomas Jefferson, a highly successful investment coveted by both Cornelius Vanderbilt and Ulysses S. Grant. Tom once won a $10,000 purse for his owner.

William was the son of a Connecticut governor, John Cotton Smith, who served from 1812 to 1817. William's mother was Mary Brown Smith, which made him a cousin of the abolitionist John Brown.

The couple had six children, three of whom died of diphtheria. At one point, the family was destitute, so Virginia applied to the City Mission, which provided her with $800. This allowed her to sustain the family and educate her children. Eventually, she bought back the land on Farmington Road in West Hartford that William had lost.

It was during this same period that Hartford's most famous resident was performing benefits for the City Mission. Samuel Clemens—alias Mark Twain—lectured at the Roberts Opera House and the Asylum Hill Congregational Church to raise funds for Father David Hawley's mission. It's fair to say that Clemens's generosity played a role in supporting the Smith family. Clemens lived near the Smiths on Farmington Avenue before he built his famous home at Nook Farm.

As her son Winchell Smith put it, Virginia "went into charitable work not on account of her interest in charity but because my father had been unsuccessful in business and the City Mission [enabled] her to clothe and educate her children, but she soon became more interested and continued it for the love of the work and not for the salary." Virginia was elected city missionary, the position left open by Father Hawley's death, on December 25, 1876.

THE PEST HOUSE

Before Virginia Smith arrived on the scene, Hartford's response to poverty and disease was traditional—and minimal. In 1849, eight people died of cholera in one week. All of them were Irish or black. The Hartford selectmen voted to erect a pest house near the city's almshouse. It was constructed with the materials left over from a small demolished building.

Five years later, in 1854, Hartford Hospital was commissioned. It eventually had a few cottages available for contagious patients. Yet poor people with contagious diseases were denied admission.

After a long delay, the new pest house finally opened in 1857. The facility housed those infected with measles, smallpox, diphtheria, scarlet fever and typhus. The building was located on the city's Town Farm, located in Asylum Hill (formerly Lord's Hill). It was a fifty-six-acre area around what is today Sigourney Square Park, a dumping ground in the 1800s for the city's paupers: the poor, indigent and sick.

The first inspection of the pest house was in January 1857 by Dr. H. Holmes. His report described the accommodations: "six rooms in tolerable condition, with a passage or hall running through the centre, and a door at each end. The stove stands in the hall. All the rooms have been sufficiently warmed for the good of the patients." A Cornish nurse attended the smallpox victims there, who received "abundant" fuel and food. This was the first and probably the last time such an inspection was ever publicized.

Indeed, other physicians hired by the town admitted they had never stepped inside the building.

The next month, Dr. Holmes reported on twenty smallpox cases he had witnessed at home and at the pest house and the vaccinations he had administered to children and adults. Six of those infected died.

By 1864, the pest house was insufficient to care for people suffering contagious diseases, but the aldermen were not inclined to incur additional expenses. When a new building proposal came before the city authorities, it was "indefinitely postponed."

On March 17, 1874, a black man in Burlington was discovered with smallpox. He was forcibly driven to Hartford by Burlington officials, dumped off on Windsor Street and later placed in the pest house. Many such suburban towns solved their health problems in this manner.

By the late 1880s, the city started selling off parcels of land from the farm, now considered desirable property. That same year, Hartford officials took up the idea once again of a replacement for the pest house. The existing facility was inadequate: seventy-eight people had occupied the six rooms during the year. Besides, the residential area was growing, and the surrounding land was becoming much more valuable. Speculators estimated that the Town Farm could be sold for $500,000 ($10.5 million today).

Of course, no one in Hartford wanted a new pest house near them. Two possible sites, one on Vine Street and the other on Cedar Hill, were considered. The Vine Street site was chosen in 1884. Men from the almshouse cleared the grounds for the new pest house.

City officials had to decide what to do with the existing structure, which was rotting and unfit for habitation. In addition, it was likely to be infected. The building was scheduled to be fumigated and demolished. Time, effort and expense were required.

Instead, the old pest house was burned down by an arsonist on Saturday, July 4, 1885, saving the city a considerable sum.

POVERTY IS THE DISEASE

Dr. O.C. Smith was the first to discover the 1891 diphtheria cases located on Commerce Street and Charles Street, in the city's poorest neighborhoods. He attempted to have the children moved to Hartford Hospital, which had accommodations for contagious patients. Although it was not full, the hospital refused, even when a member of the hospital's executive committee pleaded with the facility's officials.

When typhus (also known as "ship's fever" or "jail fever") arrived in the city, the hospital once more refused to admit a young Italian boy who had contracted the disease. The hospital's own cottages for contagion were not full, but apparently they were reserved for patients who could pay. What other reason was there for denying care to the poor patients?

Virginia Smith did not condemn those who created the economic conditions that caused poverty and crime. But she understood the connection nevertheless.

Her analysis and practice led her from traditional charitable functions to remedies and prevention, especially for children. "The expense to the community of prevention will be far less than that of any attempt at care in all the moral diseases caused by the poverty, ignorance or vicious surroundings of its young children," she wrote. "It is a higher duty of society to prevent crime than to punish it."

When we analyze Virginia Smith's work from today's perspective, its progressive nature becomes apparent. Usually, her many endeavors are categorized as "charity." Yet there is much more to the innovative projects that came from her vision.

Smith's early employment bureau was much like a utopian scheme known as a "time store," where women with specific skills would trade their work to other women. For example, a seamstress would make garments for a laundress, who would wash the needlewoman's clothes. Her "loan system" was much like a current credit union. Families with a disabled breadwinner could count on a "nurse corps" like today's home health care aides. The "Sister Dora Society" became a community center where women could learn literacy skills. Her voluntary kindergartens evolved into public daycare and kindergartens across the state.

Efforts we now simply consider social services were unique, radical and visionary acts that crossed class and racial lines. Before Virginia Smith, they did not exist in Hartford.

A RIGHT TO LIVE AND WORK

After her death, Virginia Smith was recognized for her groundbreaking efforts on behalf of children, especially the poor and disabled. Her

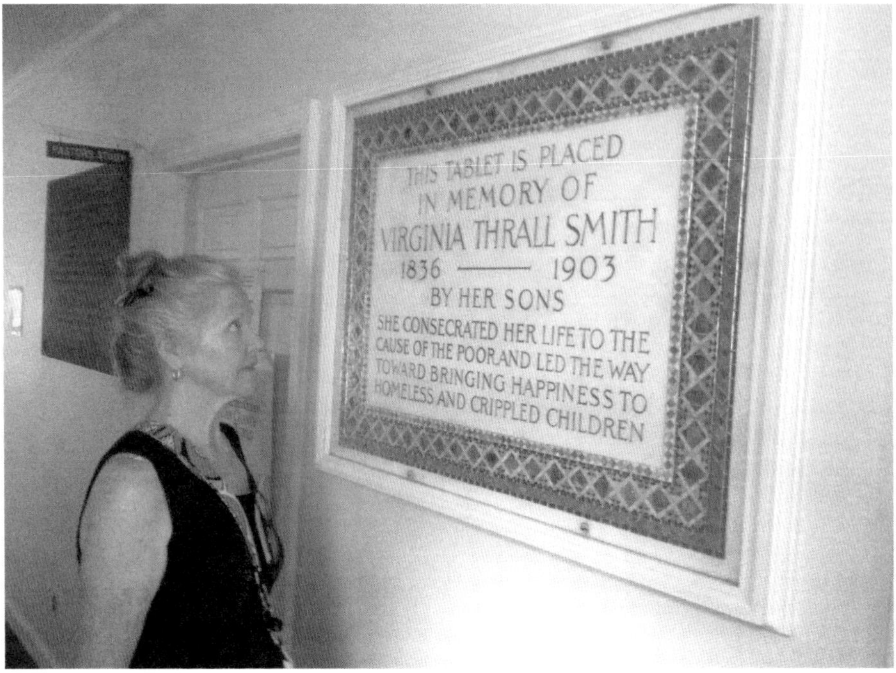

Virginia T. Smith's great-great-granddaughter Kate Butterworth Valdez. She is viewing the plaque Virginia's sons dedicated in 1915. *Author's photo.*

extraordinary work pioneered valuable institutions that neither local government nor business considered their responsibility.

For her troubles, she was slandered by cynical politicians and headline-hungry newspapers. The unfair criticism took its toll on Smith and her family. As she wrote to a friend, the suffragist Isabella Beecher Hooker, "I have a right to live and work. This fierce opposition haunts my dreams, seasons my food, burns in my heart and makes me almost lifeless at times. I do not admit it to everyone but I must acknowledge it myself that it makes the days hard and burdensome."

One of Virginia Smith's great-great-granddaughters, Kate Butterworth Valdez, lives on the land that was once the Smiths' farm, in a bungalow that housed young women in need. As a young girl, she still remembers her family's memories of Virginia and the stories of her ancestor's work.

"Even fifty years later, there was still a sad and unsettled quality to their recollections," Kate remembers. "In our family, personal honor and public service was always emphasized. My grandparents still felt hurt by the attacks, especially since they knew the criticism was unwarranted. It was a slander on the whole family."

"Virginia bucked all the trends," Kate continued, "as a woman who led an important organization, who earned a salary, and who spoke out, sometimes in opposition to powerful male politicians."

Kate's family was happy to participate in Virginia's 1994 induction into the Connecticut Women's Hall of Fame. "It was important to memorialize her life's work," Kate explained. "But it is equally important to remember how political forces tried to conspire to defeat her."

6

NO RELIEF

Grinding Poverty in the Great Depression

The Great Depression hit Hartford hard. Unlike natural disasters (like the blizzard of 1888 or the floods of 1936 and 1955), this economic crisis was years in the making.

Wealth had been accumulating in the hands of a few industrialists and financial wizards since the so-called Gilded Age of the nineteenth century. Homegrown millionaires like Morgan Bulkeley and J.P. Morgan rode their riches into the twentieth century, even as the city faced the pain of slumps and recessions.

While Hartford had many fine, generous souls, and early relief efforts were organized for the most destitute, some well-to-do citizens displayed callous disregard—and often selfish disdain—for the city's working families, who scraped just to keep food on the table.

Golden Boys Mock the Poor

The boys at the Hartford Wheel Club had a great idea: they would organize a party and dress up like poor people! On January 20, 1893, the "Hard Times Supper" was held at their club rooms on the corner of Main and Grove Streets. There was no reason to let the current economic recession ruin a good time.

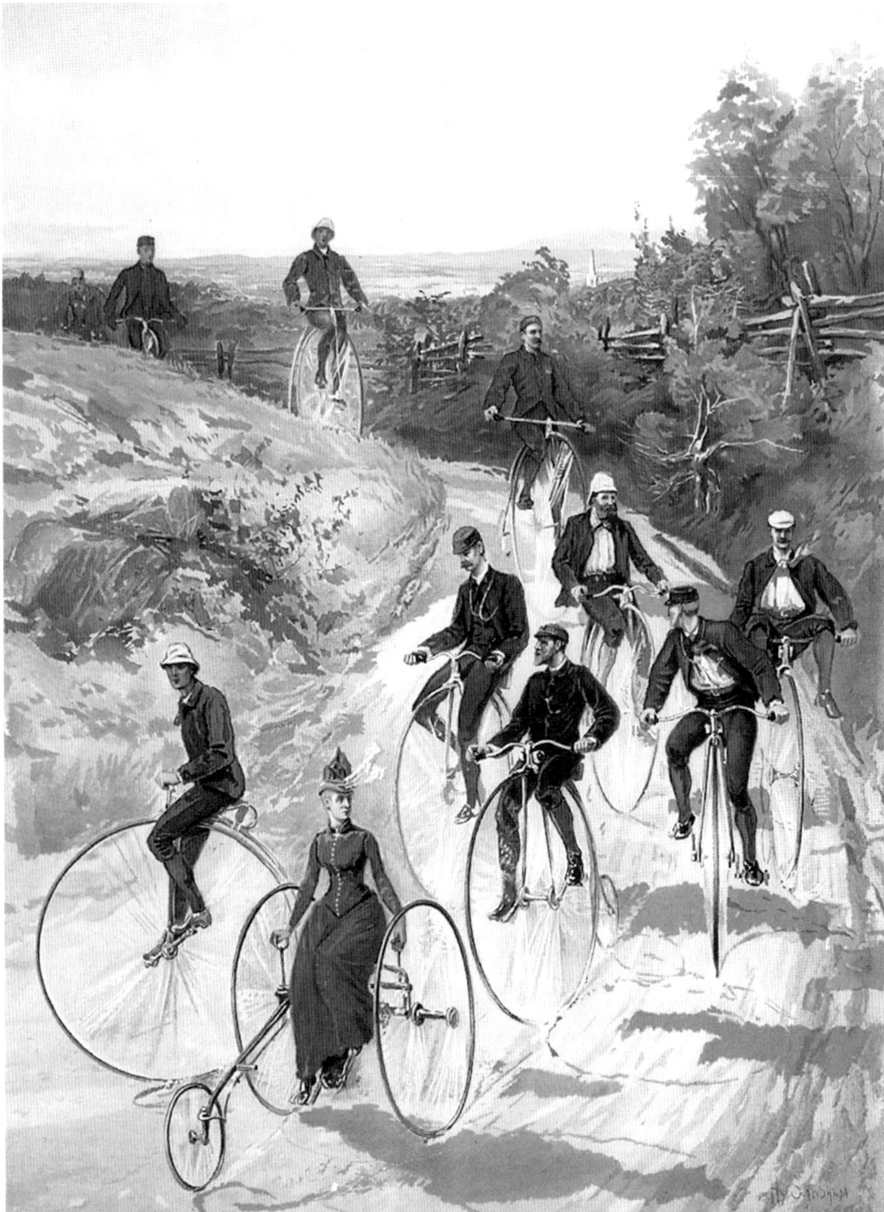

Nineteenth-century penny farthing race. *Author's collection.*

The club demanded a strict dress code for the affair: "anyone wearing a collar will be thrown out the window," warned the club's invitation. The detachable celluloid collar was a formal accessory, and only manual laborers walked around without them.

Cigars and cigarettes were forbidden, as well. Most of the poor and unemployed were not buying smokes when they couldn't feed their families. Only corncob pipes were allowed.

Four prizes were awarded for the "worst dressed" party attendees. Members of the press were asked to be judges.

The bill of fare was designed to fit the club's poverty theme. It is likely that the Wheel Club members could afford steak and champagne, but for this meal they were only offered hardtack, dried herring, cold pork and cider.

Poverty and Penny Farthings

The panic of 1893 was no joke, however. It was an era of slums, sweatshops and widespread poverty. The "Gilded Age" was a term coined by Mark Twain and served as the title of his first novel, coauthored with Charles Dudley Warner. It exposed the era's growing financial and industrial monopolies, corruption and excess wealth. It was called a "tale of golden fortune" in one newspaper review, which seemed to miss the point.

Being a dues-paying Hartford Wheel Club member was an expensive hobby. A bicycle cost $3,500 in today's dollars, equal to half a year's wages for an average workman.

In 1878, Albert Pope began to manufacture these "penny farthings"—odd-looking, high-wheeled vehicles—at his plant on Washington Street. Wheel Club members took their cycles to races in other states, which meant two- or three-day treks. Since the work week was six days (and at least sixty hours), only the leisure class could spare the time to compete.

There had been twenty-four recessions and depressions in the American economy since 1785; the last recession had hardly ended when a stock market crash, a run on the gold market and bank failures threw many thousands out of work.

MARK TWAIN'S VIEW

"Where are the poor of Hartford?" wrote Mark Twain when he first visited the city. "I confess I do not know. They are 'corralled,' doubtless—corralled in some unsanctified corner of this paradise whither my feet have not yet wondered I suppose."

He was right. The Irish immigrant population lived in poverty in the east side neighborhood known as "Pigville." Massive unemployment meant more hoboes roaming the city, which spurred the Reverend John J. McCook to lobby for restricting "tramps" to a limited section of Hartford where the almshouse was located.

The African American population was small, but job discrimination meant that black families suffered the worst housing and health conditions of any ethnic or racial group in the city.

By the time Mark Twain moved to Connecticut, *The Gilded Age* had been published and a play based on the book had been performed in Hartford. Twain championed labor unions as a means to balance the wealth gap between the "one percent" and everyone else.

As it turned out, even the Hartford Wheel Club could not escape hard times. It failed to pay the rent in October 1899; the landlord evicted the group and seized its property.

BONUS ARMY

It was a warm Sunday night in Hartford on August 7, 1932. Several dozen men and women—exhausted, dirty and hungry—trudged into the city after a hard trip from Washington, D.C. Along with 45,000 other military veterans and their families, they had camped for several months—without success—to press the government for aid.

Specifically, they wanted the immediate release of cash payments (the Bonus) promised to them after World War I. They failed: the so-called Bonus Army could not compel the Senate and President Warren Harding to vote for the pay.

These were the Depression years, with a 25 percent jobless rate and two million men and boys walking the roads or hopping freight trains in search of work. Many of the unemployed were workers-turned-soldiers who had expected jobs when they returned from European battlefields.

It's a historical fact we don't care to acknowledge: when workers are hurt by economic crises, veterans suffer more. At the turn of the twentieth century, Civil War veterans were still being found dead in Connecticut's forests and alleys. Coroners cited alcoholism or exposure, but often the real killer was society neglecting its own. By 1932, calls for social insurance, healthcare and guaranteed income were getting louder.

Navy veteran Harry Bendell of Hartford was first to call for an outdoor meeting of local veterans to join the growing protest in Washington. Local supporters donated food, gas, oil and tires to help them on their way. Cash donations allowed some unemployed workers to register their cars so they could be legally driven. Vets collected money at local baseball games and set up a headquarters across from South Green.

Even though the 1924 Bonus law passed by Congress stipulated that veterans could not receive their payout until 1945, across the country they were demanding it immediately. The veterans' rationale was persuasive:

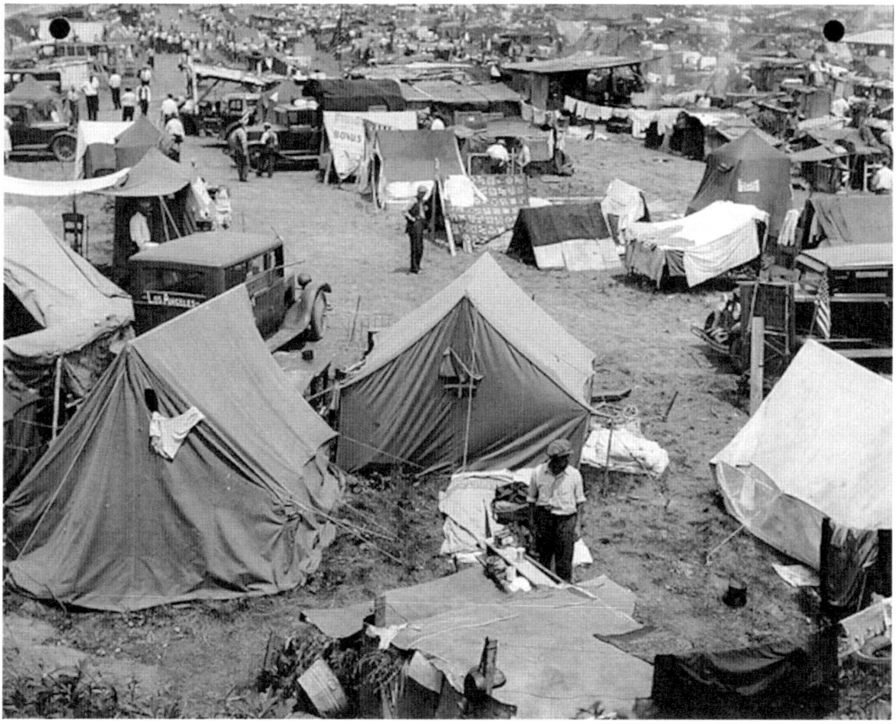

Bonus Army camp in Washington, D.C., July 1932. *Theodor Holydczak, Library of Congress, ppmsca-05577.*

soldiers had been paid thirty-three dollars a month while in the army, and the bonus was the difference between their pay and what they would have earned as factory workers back home.

The vets contrasted their plight with the U.S. munitions industrialists who had made billions of dollars, "a despicable group of citizenry who waxed rich while America's manhood groveled in the filth and corruption of the battlefield," argued Arthur Pease, a disabled veteran.

On June 12, more than 235 vets left the city's South Green for the nation's capital. To those who opposed the massive protest and insisted on more passive methods of lobbying, Simon Kaplan, a tailor, replied, "We tried writing." They were accused of disloyalty, to which veteran Joe Loveland said, "I'm not ashamed to ask for something I earned. As for being disloyal, I have an honorable discharge that says different."

Connecticut governor Wilbur Cross did not help the veterans' cause. He argued that the vets would spread disease in the Washington camps. He warned that if the Bonus was won, it could hurt the state's own veteran aid program. The state's veterans resented these tightfisted attitudes. "The very financiers who had gigantic interests are now hooting the bewildered veteran, stifling his protests for a just hearing," wrote John Clyde Williams of Hartford.

AN ARMY WITHOUT GUNS

Hartford's Bonus contingent arrived in Washington on June 14. Their food and shelter were delayed in Baltimore thanks to a truck breakdown. They slept in their cars on the first night and welcomed food from the Danbury delegation. The state veterans' camp was soon up and running, however, and well integrated into the tent city that was being built before their eyes.

The Bonus Army paraded through the streets and packed the congressional galleries to maintain a high profile. The constant activity also helped the men keep their promise that they would drink no liquor while part of the encampment.

Harry Bendell returned to Hartford briefly, where he picked up more donations, including the proceeds from a newspaper the veterans were producing and selling. Leon Boniface, a tobacco store owner, lent Bonus supporters an empty storefront at 33 Albany Avenue for the dozen volunteer staff who canvassed Hartford's neighborhoods. Pete Haverlic from Bloomfield donated two large pigs. An unnamed woman donated a brand-new cot with mattress and bedding. Bendell continued to recruit marchers and left with thirty-six more men.

Authorities were so frightened by this nonviolent army that there were three agencies spying on the movement: the local D.C. police, the army's Military Intelligence Division (MID) and J. Edgar Hoover's FBI. Hoover, predictably, said the movement was communist-dominated and that many of the demonstrators had criminal records and were not even veterans. Confidential reports listed Darien, Bridgeport and Hartford as "centers of subversive unrest."

The House passed the Bonus bill on June 16, but the Senate voted it down the next day. President Herbert Hoover had already stated that he would veto any Bonus payments. Despite the serious blow, most of the men stayed at the camps.

Without warning, on July 28, General Douglas MacArthur led hundreds of U.S. troops on horseback and in tanks to destroy the tent city. With tear gas and guns, they evicted the veterans and their families and set fire to their makeshift homes. Two vets were killed and many were injured.

It took four more years for this army without guns to win its demand.

THE UNEMPLOYED BUILD AN AIRPORT

Brainard Field may well be the country's first municipal airport. Located in a former cow pasture in southeast Hartford, Brainard opened in 1921. The era's greatest aviators—Amelia Earhart and Charles Lindbergh—landed there to wide acclaim.

During its first decade, the airfield was used primarily for passenger flights. But in 1933, as the Great Depression tightened its grip, city officials decided that Brainard should accommodate commercial traffic to spur the economy. This would require expansion and the grass airstrip runways to give way to blacktop pavement.

How could the work be done on the cheap? With the city's ever-growing number of jobless workers, of course. City employees who drove ash wagons had already been replaced by jobless men. In August 1933, the city's public welfare department advertised for the Brainard project. One hundred workers were hired. Most were family men, now desperate for jobs. They

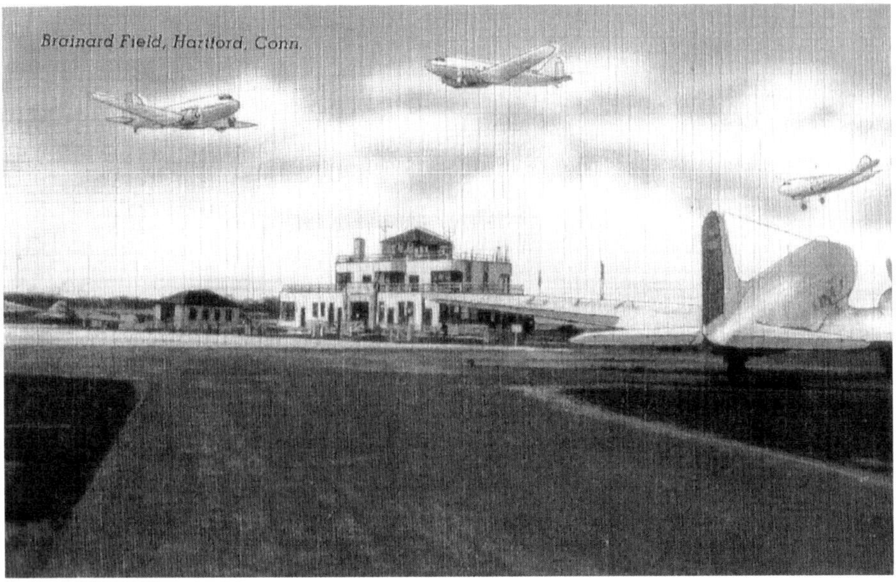

Brainard Airport, the country's oldest municipal airfield. *Author's collection.*

had worked in local factories as machinists, assemblers, laborers and office clerks before the massive layoffs occurred.

The unemployed men had heard they were to be paid forty cents an hour. Unfortunately for them, there were no wages, only food and partial rent subsidies.

Work started at 7:30 am. Most of the men had to walk three or more miles to reach the airfield. They were told that if they did not have sufficient food for lunch they should ask a private charity to assist them. Married men without children were restricted to working a maximum of two and a half days a week. Men with four or more children were allowed to work five and a half days a week.

THE STIGMA OF RELIEF

The jobs were "compulsory," announced Hartford welfare superintendent William J. Ryan. If any of the men were hired but then refused to work and later applied for public assistance, they would be arrested for nonsupport.

This program would give the men "the opportunity to regain their self-respect," Ryan declared, with no apparent irony.

The men had a different view. "I can't work for nothing," complained one. "I have to make payments on furniture." Others spoke of insurance premiums to meet, doctor bills to pay, kids' clothing to buy. "Now all we need are a ball and chain," observed one man.

"Conditions like that are enough to turn anyone into a radical," another worker said.

Federal relief programs were still several years away. Most welfare, as meager as it was, came from local sources. The popular theory was to make public assistance as difficult as possible to obtain in order to discourage dependence. Welfare violated the American spirit of pride and self-sufficiency, according to policy makers.

Outright denial of support by the government wasn't necessary, the noted sociologist Frances Fox Piven has written. If receiving aid was made degrading enough, recipients would be stigmatized and try to avoid accepting the dole. Early in the Brainard dispute, Hartford mayor Walter Batterson warned that if the men were paid wages, they would buy alcohol instead of providing for their families.

"Something to Show for Our Work"

The day after the project had begun, as word spread that there would be no wages at all, dozens of men threw down their picks and shovels. A strike was on.

The action was led by former railroad man Martin Meaney and by Will Thomas, an African American mechanic. They were supported by a multiracial committee and quickly met with Mayor Batterson. "We like to feel that no matter how small the wages, we have something to show for our work," one committeeman told him.

The dispute was settled when the mayor guaranteed that no one would be arrested for refusing the outdoor work. The men agreed to one dollar a day plus their food and rent assistance. Two buses from Main and Gold Streets would transport them to and from the job site each day.

But when the airstrip was finished, the men were unemployed once again. In these first years of the Great Depression, the Hartford Open Hearth shelter gave out ten thousand meals a year—mostly doughnuts and oatmeal—to unemployed men twice a day.

Hartford's Dismal Record

Like the rest of the country, the 1929 stock market crash meant disaster for this city's working families. As the crisis deepened, wages were cut in half for those who still had jobs, evictions were common, children suffered malnutrition and sometimes starvation. No existing institutions were capable of handling the misery caused by the economic catastrophe—not the government, not the church. Charities were overwhelmed. Even most labor unions failed to react effectively to the crisis.

And industry's response? The head of the Manufacturers' Association, E. Kent Hubbard, spoke out against local initiatives to provide old-age pensions for those who could no longer work. Such a plan would throw Connecticut into bankruptcy, Hubbard argued. The businessman's solution was to improve the local almshouses and boardinghouses.

Hartford city government had a dismal record of aiding those who needed relief. Just a few years before the crash, the mayor had spoken against using public land to create community gardens so the unemployed could feed themselves. He argued that small grocers would be hurt, but he couldn't explain how workers without income could buy at the market.

By 1933, Hartford's welfare agency was in the middle of a scandal—the department head thought that "full employment" meant he should hire his brother and friends from out of state.

Self-Sufficiency

Since Connecticut's jobless could not rely on leadership from their elected officials, they organized themselves. Unemployed Councils sprang up in cities throughout the state, often led by communists and socialists. In their ranks were the working people most affected by the crash, men and women, black and white.

Their leaders included Hartford's Joseph Laskar. On more than one occasion in those years, he and others surrounded the state capitol to demand government action. Hartford native Ernie DeMaio, who would become one of the founders of the militant United Electrical (UE) workers' union, first became active in a New York unemployed council. His job was to reconnect the gas lines for tenants who had been cut off.

THE HUNGER MARCHERS

One rallying point for Hartford's unemployed was the 1933 campaign to require the state to provide $12 million in funds for hungry Connecticut families. The general assembly's judiciary committee was scheduled to hear various relief measures, including House Bill Number 4, as the proposed fund was known.

When the committee decided to postpone the hearing for two weeks, local groups from Stamford, Bridgeport, New Haven and other cities protested, and the lawmakers reluctantly agreed to hear the bill. Hundreds of unemployed men and women began their trek to Hartford on March 20.

On the day before the hearing, hunger marchers assembled at the intersection of Main and Windsor Streets. More than four hundred people heard speakers, including Joseph Laskar, explain the need to provide immediate relief along with the establishment of unemployment insurance as a safety net for those who had jobs. In addition, Bill Number 4 demanded the end to evictions, special attention to ex-soldiers and the elimination of relief aid discrimination toward black workers.

Later that night, at the Sons of Italy Hall on Main and Sheldon Streets, hundreds of participants sang "Solidarity Forever" (labeled "a Communist anthem" by one newspaper reporter) and spoke out about the conditions in their cities. When the event ended, they braved the cold and slept in pitched tents erected in spots around the city.

The next morning, marchers rose and assembled at three locations near Bellevue Street, Zion Street and Franklin Avenue. On their way to the capitol, the workers rallied at noon at Hartford City Hall. Twenty-seven cities and towns were represented. Speakers criticized government at all levels for failing to provide for people's needs. Their signs read "We Won't Starve Quietly," "Free Milk, Hot Lunches and Clothes for Our School Children" and "We Want Food, Not War."

From city hall, they marched to the capitol. When they arrived, the marchers found the doors barred by the state police. They sang and chanted in the cold until they were allowed inside. The governor said he was sick and couldn't attend. The lieutenant governor and the Speaker of the House made similar excuses.

By the time they were allowed to testify, hundreds of hunger marchers had crowded into the judiciary committee hearing room. The proposed bill, said one speaker, was "as drastic as our needs." The marchers demanded that the $12 million appropriation for workers' relief should be derived by taxing utility companies, instituting a state income tax and diverting funds that were being spent for military training.

Their bill was defeated, and it took several years for Washington to provide the relief that local officials couldn't—or wouldn't—provide to the victims of the Great Depression.

7

DAVID AND GOLIATH

Birdsall vs. Bulkeley

In the late nineteenth century, Morgan G. Bulkeley was Connecticut's most powerful man. He served as a Hartford city councilman and alderman, as mayor, as governor and two terms as a U.S. senator. During most of this period—forty-three years—he was also the president of Aetna Insurance Company. Bulkeley was not a man you would want as an enemy.

Daniel C. Birdsall, on the other hand, was the "anti-Bulkeley." Bulkeley, a distinguished-looking WASP Republican, hailed from an old, well-connected family. Birdsall was an Irish American Democrat, just over five feet tall, a descendant of immigrants and not nearly as financially secure.

After he took on Bulkeley, Birdsall was arrested, sued, had his office demolished and his printing press confiscated. He was savagely beaten by his opponents and almost murdered. But he never backed down.

He held several jobs: a lawyer and a New York political operative, a state legislator from Westport and, eventually, the publisher of the *Hartford Telegram*.

Birdsall was more of a gadfly than a "vampire" or "dictator," names he was called by his detractors. Daniel Birdsall shook many a patrician off his perch as the owner of the *Telegram* from 1883 to 1889. He wrote and printed the most outrageous stories about Morgan Bulkeley and Hartford's rich and famous. Some of them were even true.

Judge Birdsall (he liked to be called by his title from years past) bought the *Telegram* in 1883. There was already plenty of fierce press competition; other

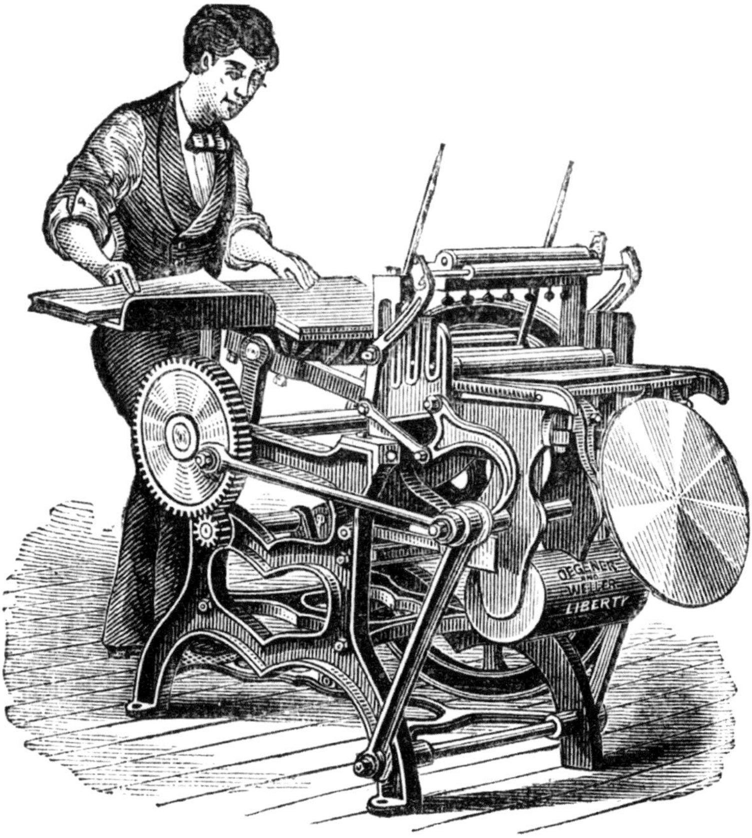

A printer and his press. *Author's collection.*

papers in Hartford at the time included the *Courant,* the *Times,* the *Post,* the *Weekly Examiner* and the *Sunday Globe*.

The term "yellow journalism" was not yet known to the reading public, but it applied to the *Telegram* under Birdsall. The description would take hold some ten years later, when William Randolph Hearst printed sensational stories that led to the label's use. Birdsall's style may have been a model for Hearst and his rival, Joseph Pulitzer.

In the written history of Birdsall versus Bulkeley, the latter appears as a statesman, the victim of an unscrupulous publisher's smears. But what has been memorialized as truth is not the whole story.

Truth, after all, is the "ingenious compound of desirability and appearance," according to Ambrose Bierce, a journalist who was a contemporary of the feuding duo.

TAXING THE 1 PERCENT

It was not simply a personality dispute between Bulkeley and Birdsall. While both men had big egos and a desire for personal power, the two had political views that were diametrically opposed. Just months before Birdsall moved to Hartford, he was a state legislator from Westport. It was during this time that he offered a tax reform bill that was astonishing for its progressivity and sure to annoy Connecticut's wealthy patricians, especially Morgan Bulkeley.

This was the Gilded Age, after all, when financial and industrial power was concentrated in the hands of a small percentage of society. Birdsall's proposed bill would tax Connecticut railroads, which were "escaping taxation to the detriment of the entire people," he charged. Birdsall argued that no rail syndicate should make a 45 percent profit. If it did, "there is a big steal somewhere."

His plan included taxing the insurance companies, banks, trust companies, express steamboat companies and telephone and telegraph concerns. All told, Birdsall calculated, the tax would raise more than $15 million annually. The Republican-controlled legislature squashed the bill.

BIRDSALL THE POPULIST

The scrappy newspaper made its reputation on a variety of subjects. The *Telegram* published straight through the Blizzard of '88, providing information and news each day about the conditions, including the names of those stranded in hotels, the availability of food and transportation into the city.

On November 2, 1887, Birdsall reported on the public outcry against the danger of railroad crossings, which were the scene of many fatal accidents. A recent measure had been taken by the state legislature to correct them. Twenty-two of the crossings in eleven towns were repaired, partially at public expense, with the bulk of the cost applied to the train companies. There were still more to fix and many more carriages and pedestrians to protect.

Birdsall noted that the New England rail line was owned by the Standard Oil Company, none of whose stockholders lived in Connecticut. Yet a majority of the state senate wanted to shift most of the repair costs to the public. Birdsall warned that the railroad syndicate would be inclined "to bring such wealth to bear on the lower house" that the state might be compelled "to bear seventy-five percent of all the costs."

Although he was active in Irish nationalist politics, Birdsall didn't hesitate to attack the city's "Home Rule" organization for a fundraiser at which more than a thousand tickets were sold. (Home rule was an Irish demand for more political power from their British colonial masters.) He noted a wide discrepancy between the number of seats filled and the ticket revenue and challenged the group's leaders to explain the difference. As it turned out, Morgan Bulkeley had organized (manipulated, Birdsall charged) the vote to become the leader of the local group.

Birdsall championed the work of the city missionary's office, run by Virginia Thrall Smith. He allowed her to write a column that he printed on the front page. She used the opportunity to squash a false rumor that she opposed consolidation of private charities. In fact, she wrote, she was in full support of coordinating their work and listed her many partners, including the YMCA and YWCA.

The *Telegram* spoke out against the gambling racket that flourished in Hartford and was "robbing the poor daily out of hundreds of dollars." When a member of the city council proposed a bill to tighten control over "policy playing" (much like today's lottery), it was shelved by Mayor Bulkeley, who said that the existing state law was sufficient.

"No one has yet been discovered who has ever won at the game except the proprietors," Birdsall wrote. The newspaper started its own crusade, exposing how businessmen played the numbers by using messenger boys to bring payments to a room on the second floor of 104 Asylum Street. He also named Gold Street and Front Street taverns as gambling outlets.

Those who played the policy game were being "fleeced," Birdsall warned. "There was scarcely anyone among the lower classes who did not have some pitiful tale of a friend or relation a slave to the fascinating game."

But it wasn't only working people who were taken in. "The policy shop has found its way to the aristocratic drawing room, and it has reached the proportions of a craze among fashionable ladies in the city," the *Telegram* reported. "A number of them send their pocket money down by the coachman every morning and he places it as directed."

"The policy shops must go!" Birdsall demanded, almost as a direct challenge to Mayor Bulkeley. This was not the last time Daniel Birdsall would stand in opposition to Bulkeley.

SCANDAL IN CHICAGO

In June 1884, Mayor Bulkeley and other leaders of the Connecticut Republican Party traveled to Chicago for the party's convention to choose a presidential candidate and adopt a platform (which, among other things, supported the exclusion of Chinese labor into the country).

Birdsall knew that there was a story in Chicago beyond delegate horse-trading. He hired a private detective to follow the Bulkeley group. What he found was extremely embarrassing to the head of Aetna Life Insurance Company: Bulkeley and his cohorts lodged in one of the city's most distinguished houses of prostitution. When they absolutely had to be present at the convention, horse-drawn cabs were on standby. Birdsall promptly published what his detective found.

Birdsall also charged that Bulkeley used Aetna company funds for his illegal activities in Chicago. Bulkeley vehemently denied this, stating that he spent his own money. This became his defense against the whorehouse revelations.

The private dick returned with sworn statements from cab drivers and from Carrie Watson, the madam of the house. It all added up to a monumental mortification for this pillar of society.

BIRDSALL THE SENSATIONALIST

Daniel Birdsall was not above uncovering and printing crime stories that other newspapers wouldn't touch. The reports and accompanying headlines could be lurid. In just one week, Birdsall published the following:

> *"A RAVING MANIAC. Damnable Crime Committed in a Road House. A Hartford Girl Decoyed, Drugged and Outraged."* (11/3/87)

"PRETTY MAIDENS. Smile While They Induce the Unwary to Purchase. Fair Given by the First Baptist Church Young People." (11/5/87)

"MURDER AND ARSON. John Hodel Shoots His Wife at Hebron. And Then Sets Fire to the House." (11/8/87)

But the *Telegram's* pages were not just printing ugly stories. The paper also covered international news, "feel good" items and sports stories. One light-hearted headline reported the sound beating a Meriden baseball team took from the Hartford Kangaroos: "Sandville Sluggers Slaughtered by Sloopville Scientists."

Birdsall also liked to tweak the well-established papers that held plenty of sway in local politics. Foremost among his targets was the *Hartford Courant.* When the *Telegram* printed two exclusive crime stories in a row, Birdsall crowed that as his paper "recorded scoop after scoop, the Old Man With The Whiskers fairly made the air blue with expletives."

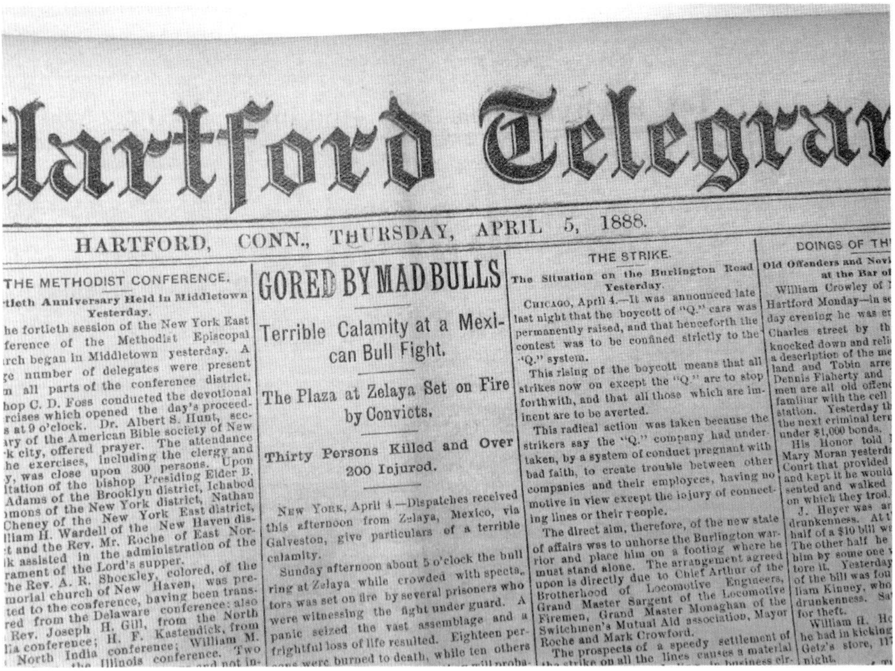

Hartford Telegram

HARTFORD, CONN., THURSDAY, APRIL 5, 1888.

THE METHODIST CONFERENCE.

Fortieth Anniversary Held in Middletown Yesterday.

The fortieth session of the New York East Conference of the Methodist Episcopal Church began in Middletown yesterday. A large number of delegates were present from all parts of the conference district. Bishop C. D. Foss conducted the devotional exercises which opened the day's proceedings at 9 o'clock. Dr. Albert S. Hunt, secretary of the American Bible society of New York city, offered prayer. The attendance at the exercises, including the clergy and laity, was close upon 300 persons. Upon invitation of the bishop Presiding Elder B. Adams of the Brooklyn district, Ichabod Simmons of the New York district, Nathan Cheney of the New York East district, William H. Wardell of the New Haven district and the Rev. Mr. Roche of East Norwalk assisted in the administration of the sacrament of the Lord's supper.

The Rev. A. R. Shockley, colored, of the Memorial church of New Haven, was presented to the conference, having been transferred from the Delaware conference; also Rev. Joseph H. Gill, from the North India conference; H. F. Kastendick, from the North India conference; William M. ... the Illinois conference. Two ... and not in-

GORED BY MAD BULLS

Terrible Calamity at a Mexican Bull Fight.

The Plaza at Zelaya Set on Fire by Convicts.

Thirty Persons Killed and Over 200 Injured.

NEW YORK, April 4.—Dispatches received this afternoon from Zelaya, Mexico, via Galveston, give particulars of a terrible calamity.

Sunday afternoon about 5 o'clock the bull ring at Zelaya while crowded with spectators was set on fire by several prisoners who were witnessing the fight under guard. A panic seized the vast assemblage and a frightful loss of life resulted. Eighteen persons were burned to death, while ten others ... will proba-

THE STRIKE.

The Situation on the Burlington Road Yesterday.

CHICAGO, April 4.—It was announced late last night that the boycott of "Q." cars was permanently raised, and that henceforth the contest was to be confined strictly to the "Q." system.

This rising of the boycott means that all strikes now on except the "Q." are to stop forthwith, and that all those which are imminent are to be averted.

This radical action was taken because the strikers say the "Q." company had undertaken, by a system of conduct pregnant with bad faith, to create trouble between other companies and their employees, having no motive in view except the injury of connecting lines or their people.

The direct aim, therefore, of the new state of affairs was to unhorse the Burlington warrior and place him on a footing where he must stand alone. The arrangement agreed upon is directly due to Chief Arthur of the Brotherhood of Locomotive Engineers, Grand Master Sargent of the Locomotive Firemen, Grand Master Monaghan of the Switchmen's Mutual Aid association, Mayor Roche and Mark Crowford.

The prospects of a speedy settlement of the strike on all the lines causes a material ... in business cir-

DOINGS OF TH...

Old Offenders and Novi... at the Bar of ...

William Crowley of ... Hartford Monday—in ... day evening he was ... Charles street by th... knocked down and reli... a description of the me... land and Tobin arre... Dennis Flaherty and ... men are all old offend... familiar with the cell ... station. Yesterday th... the next criminal term ... under $1,000 bonds.

His Honor told ... Mary Moran yesterd... Court that provided ... and kept it he would ... sented and walked ... on which they trod.

J. Heyer was ar... drunkenness. At t... half of a $10 bill w... The other half he ... him by some one ... tore it. Yesterday ... of the bill was fou... liam Kinney, who ... drunkenness. Sa... for theft.

William H. H... he had in kicking ... Getz's store, 11... night.

Front page of the *Hartford Telegram*, 1888. *Author's photo.*

Writing like a fly on the wall at the *Courant's* newsroom, Birdsall exclaimed, "[T]here has been more real fun on the top floor of the big brick building for the past few days than at any time within the 123 years of the old lady's existence."

BULKELEY EXPLODES

Morgan Bulkeley served as Hartford's mayor from 1880 to 1888. He expected to go out with a bang, straight into the governor's office. In April, at the end of his term, Bulkeley prepared to deliver his final speech to the city council. But in the days before Bulkeley's farewell, there was Birdsall yapping at his heels.

First, the *Telegram* accused Bulkeley's government of running up a deficit while in office and questioned what some others must have been thinking: how would Bulkeley balance a much larger state budget? There were disputes about the charges against Bulkeley. The fact that there were two budgets, one for the Town of Hartford and one for the City of Hartford, made the whole thing confusing. (For instance, the town collected all the revenues from liquor licenses, but the city had to fund the police, which was tasked with maintaining the peace against booze-related crimes.)

The *Hartford Times* promptly published the *Telegram*'s findings, which more than doubled the bad publicity for Bulkeley. All his planning for a smooth, triumphant exit as mayor was ruined. Consequently, he was reported to have spent most of his speech railing against Birdsall and the *Telegram*. Clearly unnerved, Bulkeley even embarrassed some of his own loyal supporters with his burst of anger.

AETNA CANCELS THE FIRST AMENDMENT

After his exposé of Bulkeley's Chicago shenanigans, on July 2, 1888, the *Telegram* charged that Aetna's financial status was shaky. This was the last straw and provided an opening for Bulkeley.

At about 3:00 p.m., Bulkeley and the city marshall walked into the *Telegram* office on State Street with a written complaint from Aetna. They "proceeded to demolish our office and to take away the entire plant," according to Birdsall. Morgan Bulkeley was clearly in control, and he had the printing press and equipment stored in the basement of Aetna. Birdsall was arrested.

But he was undaunted. The next day, Birdsall published and distributed a broadside exclaiming that the *Telegram* was very much alive. He reprinted his Aetna charges in the broadside. He was arrested again.

Bulkeley had him arrested a third time, bringing a civil action against Birdsall for the same libel claim.

Did Bulkeley and law enforcement have any legal right to shut down the *Telegram* for alleged libel? It seems outrageous now, more like the act of a dictator than of someone who defends American liberty.

At the time, several Hartford newspapers embraced the shutdown and confiscation as a perfectly acceptable move. This says more about Bulkeley's power than it does about other editors' support for the First Amendment.

The *National Law Review* took notice, however. The prestigious journal noted the confiscation as an unusual response to a libel charge: "The Hartford Telegram Company was sued by Aetna Insurance Company for $50,000 damages for libel, and the plaintiff, instead of putting a keeper in charge of the attachment, as usual, completely gutted the office of furniture, type and fixtures, thereby preventing any issue of the paper until the amount as settled." This is where most accounts of Daniel Birdsall's Hartford adventures conclude. But it's not where his story ends.

MURDEROUS INTENT

On November 14, 1888, a Wednesday night, three men attacked Daniel Birdsall as the publisher was walking near his Park Street office. Lucien Smith, Allen Wiley and Henry Hall used whips, their fists and a pistol to assault Birdsall, who ultimately escaped.

The men later said they were incensed about an allegation Birdsall had printed a few days earlier, calling the editors of the *Sunday Globe* "swindlers and blackmailers." The three worked for and edited the *Globe*.

The *Hartford Courant* immediately printed the story concocted by the attackers as if it were the facts. No attempt was made to contact Birdsall about the attack. The *Courant* headline read, "Horsewhipped. Birdsall Severely Punished." The article began, "The scurrilous paper published by D.C. Birdsall published an article of blackmail and swindling against the *Sunday Globe*." It is obvious where the *Courant* stood: Birdsall was being "punished" for his newspaper's stories.

The coverage by the *Hartford Times* was no better. The account of the attack on Birdsall was written in the style of a melodrama script, with the attackers recorded in the cast list as "The Villains."

The three men were arrested but almost immediately released from jail. Morgan Bulkeley provided the full $75,000 bail to get them released—almost $2 million in today's money. Birdsall wasted no time suing the *Sunday Globe*.

There were charges and countercharges. In their defense, the men argued that the smearing of someone's good name was justification for the beating. Their lawyers spent a great deal of effort showing how the *Telegram* printed highly charged accusations against various others, including governor-elect Bulkeley. Their defense also hinged on the accusation that Birdsall fired the gun.

The presiding judge didn't buy it. On November 20, Judge William F. Henney described the testimony of several witnesses whom he credited with an accurate account of the assault:

> [The witness Woodward] *states that he stood in a doorway not far from Birdsall; that standing there he noticed the defendant, Smith, standing with his arm extended in the direction of Birdsall, who was thirty to thirty-five feet away from Smith, saw the flash of what he believed to be a pistol in Smith's hand and heard the report; that just before the shooting heard Wiley say to Smith "don't fire" or "don't shoot;" that after the shot was fired, he saw Smith put something in the inside of his overcoat, button it up and start away in the direction of Main Street.*
>
> *Two boys corroborated this witness by stating that at the time of the firing they were west of Birdsall and about twenty feet from him, and that he was then walking in their direction with his back toward his assailants, and that the shot came from behind him and from the east of him.*
>
> *One of those boys claims to have been hit by this pistol ball, and exhibited in court a bullet taken the next day from the collar of his coat. As the evidence stands I am led to the conclusion that the shot was not fired by Birdsall, but by one of the attacking parties.*
>
> *Smith admits that Woodward correctly states that he* [Smith] *was standing a short distance from Birdsall with his arm extended, but claims that he had a whip and not a pistol, and that he neither shot nor saw any flash of a weapon....In the melee a pistol shot is fired and an unoffending child narrowly escapes injury.*

> *The evidence on this, as it seems to me, is strongly against the defendant. The transaction itself is, from beginning to end, a disgrace to Hartford. It lacks even the excuse of being a fair fight. A man past middle life is waylaid in a public street by three young men and beaten, according to a prearranged plan. Nor is this done in the heat of passion, but some days after the article occasioning the assault had been published.*

The judge went on to say, essentially, that if anyone was aggrieved by Birdsall's charges, they could take the matter to court but could not "avenge their own private grievances."

MORGAN BULKELEY'S INVISIBLE HAND?

The incident leading up to Birdsall's attempted murder was a dispute between two newspapers, the *Telegram* and the *Globe*. Morgan Bulkeley was neither a defendant nor an accuser. Apparently, his only public connection to the trial was the $2 million he put up for the three attackers.

That makes the resolution of Birdsall's legal cases all the more interesting. On March 13, 1889, Birdsall's attackers were found guilty and given small fines. Simultaneously, he dropped complaints made against the *Globe* men, and Bulkeley dropped his charges of libel against Birdsall. In contrast to the extensive coverage given to the attackers (which proved to be false), the final legal report was terse:

> *THE BIRDSALL CASES.*
> *All Now Disposed of—Wiley and Smith Fined $10 each for Assault.*
>
> *In the superior court yesterday morning Allen Wiley and Lucien P. Smith pleaded guilty to assault on D.C. Birdsall and were fined $10 and costs each. The charges of assault against Henry, and of assault with intent to kill against Lucien P. Smith, all based on the Birdsall affair, were nolled by the state attorney. Mr. Birdsall having refused to press his suit for damages against those parties, and the Aetna Life Insurance company and Governor Bulkeley not desiring to press the various suits against Mr. Birdsall, all those actions have been withdrawn from the docket.*

Now, it could be just a coincidence that all these cases were settled together. It could be.

Morgan Bulkeley ran for governor in 1888. He received fewer votes than his opponent but was backed by his party and remained in the job. Most of the legislature objected to Bulkeley's occupation of the office and refused to pass a state budget. Bulkeley borrowed $300,000 (about $8 million today) from Aetna to keep the state operating.

As Connecticut historian Carl Van Dusen put it, "Public opinion seems to have been deeply aroused...by the frequent spectacle of the Assembly electing as governor a man who had received fewer votes than his opponent." A few years later, a large majority of voters determined that in the future, the highest vote-getter would win.

For a while, Daniel Birdsall stayed involved in Democratic politics and wrote for magazines like the *Century*. He died at the age of fifty-four. Bulkeley lived until the ripe old age of ninety-four, dying in 1922.

EVEN FEUDS END

Publilius Syrus was a first-century BC writer from Syria taken by the Romans as a slave. The origin of his given name can be roughly translated as "of the people," a designation both Morgan Bulkeley and Daniel Birdsall would no doubt have claimed for themselves.

Publilius wrote: "As men, we are all equal in the presence of death." Morgan Bulkeley and Daniel Birdsall are both buried in the prestigious Cedar Hill Cemetery on Fairfield Avenue in Hartford.

It has been said—or is it just a wicked rumor?—that on the Irish holiday of Samhain (Halloween), along with the faeries and the *sith*, the ghost of Daniel Birdsall rises from his grave, just to taunt Morgan Bulkeley.

8

NEWSIES, BOOTBLACKS AND TELEGRAPH BOYS

NEWSIES

The front-page photo was startling, even to people who had lived in the city all their lives. On May 4, 1909, the *Hartford Evening Post* displayed the image of an alley just a block from the Colt Firearms factory. The tenement yards were full of garbage that "reeked of a germ-laden stench."

Not surprisingly, five people had just contracted diphtheria in this Dutch Point neighborhood. Hartford was a thriving city at the start of the twentieth century, but its poor people, mostly immigrants, still struggled and suffered. Hartford children sold newspapers as a way to survive. Seven days a week, often late into the night, as many as two hundred city youngsters sold the *Post* and the other Hartford newspapers for pennies a copy.

Unfortunately for them, in 1909, the "newsies" found their meager living threatened because of a brawl between the country's most powerful newspaper moguls. Joseph Pulitzer, owner of the *New York World*, and William Randolph Hearst, who owned the *New York Evening Journal*, were constantly competing with an eye to maximizing profits.

The rivals' latest tactic was to refuse to credit distributors for unsold papers. Until this time, newsboys bought bundles of papers and would be compensated for what they couldn't sell. When the two millionaires halted the practice, it hurt the newsies' earnings. Both New York papers were popular in Hartford; several editions arrived by train each day.

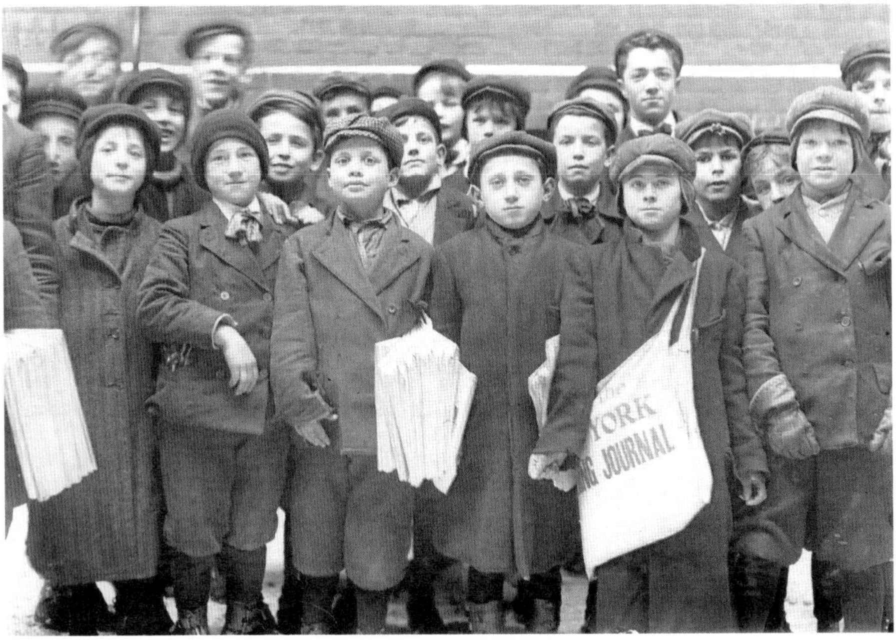

Hartford newsies at the Hartford Times building. They are carrying local papers and the afternoon New York papers that have arrived by train, March 1909. *Lewis Hine, National Child Labor Committee. Library of Congress.*

It was the job of Herman P. Koppelmann, Hearst's agent in Hartford, to implement the latest cutback. The newsies were not about to accept this reduction without a fight. On the morning of May 1, 1909, boys from all over the city met at Zion Hall on Winthrop and Pleasant Streets (where Barnard Brown School now stands). It was raining, but that didn't stop one hundred boys from marching behind a drum-and-bugle corps with a huge banner urging customers to buy only local newspapers.

The next day, the young workers formally created the Hartford Newsboys' Association. Assisting them were Sol Sontheimer of the Central Labor Union and Mary Graham Jones, the head social worker at the Hartford Social Settlement. The mass meeting elected Harry Brightman as union president and Morris Zalkowitz as vice president.

The newsies' union received significant local support. Hartford drugstores refused to stock the two New York papers, and many regular customers stopped buying them. Individuals and businesses made donations to the strike. At a second parade on May 17, the newsies were carrying flags and wearing white caps and union pins, purchased with the aid they had received.

Herman Koppelmann knew how to handle his boys, however. He had been through similar disruptions before, every time the newsboys were forced to absorb a new pay cut. Koppelmann used strikebreaking tactics that had been perfected by industrialists who faced unionization on a mass scale: he hired black residents as strikebreakers to sell papers, imported adults from out of town to intimidate the newsies (the young strikers beat them up) and spread rumors that the strike was over. Koppelmann also recruited his brother Abraham to organize an "alternative" association to compete with the boys' union.

To sow greater confusion within the newsies' ranks, Koppelmann intimated that rival New York newspapers were secretly paying strike leaders to prolong the labor dispute at the expense of the rank and file. This the boys hotly denied: "We are fully competent to handle the situation in question, which is proven by the fact that we have fought our opponents successfully for two Sundays and seven weekdays without the aid of any publisher whatsoever," wrote striker Nick Murano.

Hearst's *Journal* even sent an undercover representative to Hartford to break the strike. A local clothing store owner exposed the *Journal* man when he was discovered trying to buy a large number of boys' suits and shoes. Kopplemann had planned to offer the duds as a bribe to any striking newsie who broke ranks.

In the end, the pressure on the newsies proved too great to withstand. The leading union figures traded charges of graft, fought with each other and split their ranks. It is not known precisely what role Herman Kopplemann played in these disruptions, but the outcome served his purpose. On May 19, after three separate votes, the youngsters ended their strike.

Seven months later, the newsies learned that Herman Kopplemann was no longer the Hartford wholesale agent for Hearst's *Journal*. Instead, there was a new distributor: Harry Brightman, former newsboy union president. Harry continued to live in Hartford, raised a family and went on to become a successful used car salesman and a pillar of the community.

Kopplemann parlayed his newspaper dealership into a political career. Ironically, he became the "friend of the working man," successfully winning elections for the city council, state senate and U.S. Congress. At the Connecticut General Assembly, Koppelmann introduced pro-labor legislation, including a bill to prohibit the state militia from interfering with labor strikes. He was endorsed by the progressive Congress of Industrial Organizations (CIO) and was considered a solid New Dealer.

A newsboy's life was never easy. Consider, for example, this Hartford story:

> *Charles Brown, a tinsmith, aged 30, made an unprovoked assault on a little newsboy named Maher on High Street yesterday afternoon. Brown had stolen a paper from the boy, and when the child weepingly asked for his paper the brute threw him down and knocked his head against the sidewalk, T.W. Hannum, Jr., saw the occurrence, and interfered with the brute, and knocked him down, but not before Brown had got Hannum's hand between his teeth, and had bitten him.*
>
> *Officer Stewart arrested him, and the inhuman monster, the assailant of defenceless children, will be tried this morning on charges of mayhem and assault.*

The newsies' organizing efforts continued, but conditions only got tougher for them over the next decade. Hartford officials declared that the boys' newspaper bundles blocked sidewalk traffic and were a nuisance. The cops roughly cleared the newsies out by throwing their papers into the gutter. The city also began to require all young paper sellers to register and wear ID badges. The eventual end of the newsies was signaled when the *Hartford Times* installed street-corner vending machines, charging a nickel for every three-cent newspaper and eliminating the need for newsies altogether.

Bootblacks

A story circulated in Hartford toward the end of the nineteenth century about a young bootblack who worked on a steamship. Perhaps he found the competition on land too stiff; the number of boys working in the trade always grew when times were hard. But even the meager sum that shining shoes brought into the family could mean the difference between eating and going hungry.

As a stocky, bearded man walked by on the deck, the boy asked him if he needed a shine. The man clearly did, but the boy was polite enough not to criticize, just to inquire. The gentleman stopped and lit a cigar; the boy went to work. When he finished, he held out his hand, waiting to be paid. The man slipped him a paper bill, in a quarter-dollar denomination.

This angered the boy. He wanted coins, not a "worthless" greenback. Yes, holding paper money was a show of faith in the U.S. government, both

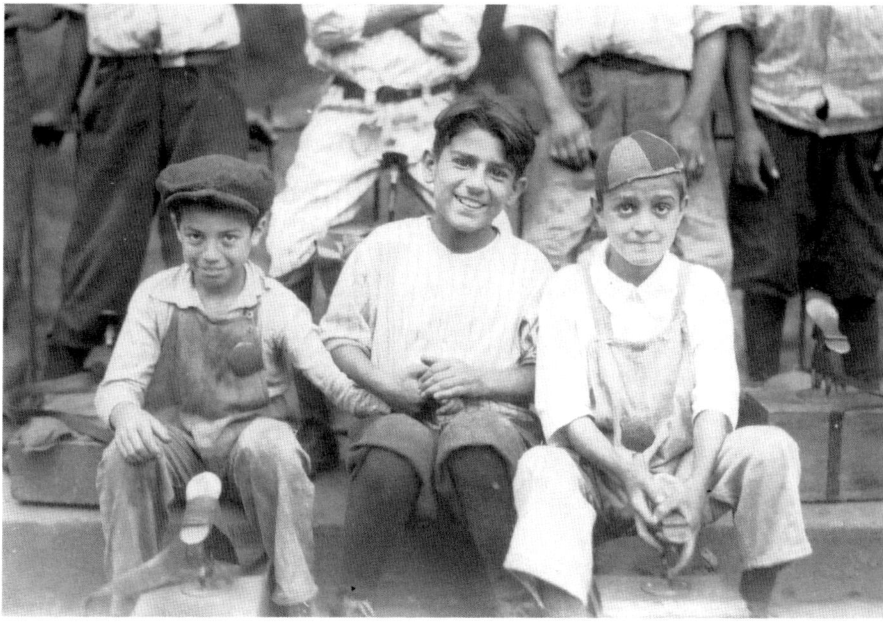

Hartford bootblacks, also known as shoeshine boys, summer 1924. *Lewis Hine, National Child Labor Committee. Library of Congress.*

during and after the Civil War. But those who hoarded gold and silver were opportunists, waiting for the North to lose the conflict or collapse altogether. Those who used paper money were optimists and patriots.

A bystander saw the boy's distress and approached him. "That was General Grant," he told the boy.

Bootblacks have long been the subject of nostalgia in American culture, with stories in the local press about colorful figures like Speck Macton and Cesar Diggs. But the reality of a bootblack's life was no quaint tale. The art of shining shoes, as poorly paid as it was, became a trade that kept working people a step ahead of poverty.

Many bootblacks formed unions for mutual protection. At a national convention in 1900 of the American Federation of Labor (AFL), one young boy took the platform to demand that the unionists clean house before passing lofty resolutions. Referring to the shoeshine services at the convention's hotel, he declared, "I want those scab bootblacks to keep out! I am a union boy and I want them put out!"

Hartford regulated the trade as far back as 1888. The city limited the number of bootblack licenses to seventeen (thirty-five ragpickers were allowed to work that year). Only one license per family was allowed. The police could arrest a bootblack without a license, and the chief could take away a boy's permit for almost any reason.

The number of bootblacks swelled when the Great Depression hit Connecticut. As unemployment increased, so did the numbers of men and boys looking for income. Bootblacks rose from 100 to 250 in Hartford alone. One boy's story typified the hardships faced by the poor of the city.

Danny D'Onofrio was twelve years old and lived with his family on Charles Street in Hartford's poorest neighborhood. His father had died; his mother was raising seven children. One of his brothers was in the hospital with a deformed spine, and one of his sisters had her own child. Danny was the main breadwinner. Like others, he worked from the morning to late at night, seven days a week. "Sometimes not all the cops pay for their shine," he told a reporter.

As the trade grew, so did the complaints against it. Italian boys waited for business in front of the post office. Men who loafed around the area would throw coins into the crowd and cheered when the boys fought over the money. Bootblacks were considered a nuisance by local businesses and the police.

The board of aldermen held hearings in July 1930 to "close downtown" to the bootblacks. Anonymous complaints alleged that the boys were guilty of "gambling, profanity, and rowdyism."

Alderman James Kennedy pointed out that a bootblack's weekly earnings were far below the average adult wage. The boys defended their livelihood at city hall. Dominic J. Curio and Sergio Gionfriddo, officers of the Hartford Boys Boot Black Association, spoke on behalf of their coworkers.

Dominic explained how he bought groceries and paid the rent for his family stuck deep in poverty. He spent seven days a week on the job and earned between six and ten dollars for a sixty- to seventy-hour workweek. In contrast, electricians made six dollars for one eight-hour day.

Dominic provided an "able defense" before the elected officials and taught the lawmakers the real conditions of poverty that festered as the Depression grew.

"If you take us off the busy streets and put us on streets that are not busy, we won't make enough to buy shoe leather," Dominic told the council. The bootblacks' younger brothers and sisters ran barefoot on the hot summer streets, he said.

Finally, in 1932, the city council accepted a plan offered by a social service group to allow bootblacks to work at designated stations around the downtown area. Taking into account the demands of local businesses, the number of shoeshine boxes were limited on certain streets. The Friends of Hartford Boys mapped out two hundred sites where from one to four bootblacks could set up shop. The plan was opposed, to no avail, by the larger, more established bootblack businesses that employed individual shoe shiners and made a profit off the boys' labor.

By 1953, the city designated 325 stations in the business district. Still visible today are some of the official "BB" marks painted on Hartford curbs.

Telegraph Boys

"I can hire one half of the working class to kill the other half," said Jay Gould, probably the most ruthless "robber baron" of the nineteenth century. It was not an idle threat. So why would a handful of Hartford telegraph workers in 1883 take him on?

Gould robbed working people and millionaires alike. He bought his way out of the Civil War draft, issued millions of dollars in phony railroad stock, bribed legislators and manipulated President Grant in an attempt to corner the gold market. Worst of all, he was a notorious union buster. Gould bought a newspaper to improve his public image, kept plainclothes police with him at all times and bomb-proofed his newly purchased New York Western Union office—with good reason. He was the industrialist the public loved to hate, the "Octopus of the Wires" as described by one of his former employees.

Toward the end of the nineteenth century, three local telegraph offices kept Hartford connected to the rest of the country: Western Union (bought by Gould in 1881), Mutual Union and American Rapid. Hartford was the largest relay office in New England outside of Boston. Fifteen lines were in constant operation, but the office had the capacity to operate sixty lines at a time. Operators, linemen, battery-men, clerks and message boys were all employed to keep the system running efficiently.

While Western Union's profits had greatly increased over the previous decade, telegraph workers' wages had actually been cut and their hours increased. On July 19, 1883, a nationwide strike began. Hartford, New Haven and Norwich operators joined the effort.

Telegraph work was arduous, as even the former president of Western Union admitted to a congressional committee. William Orton testified that

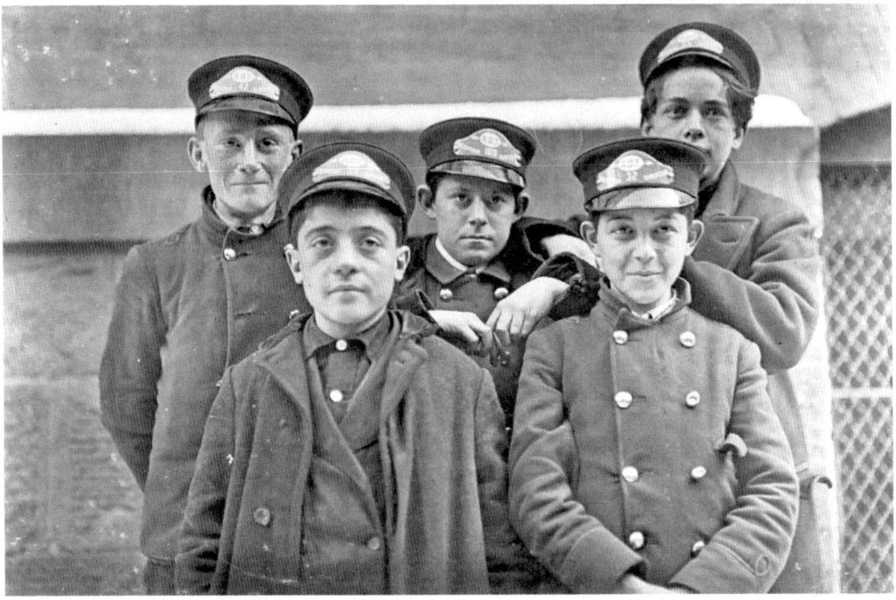

Hartford boys employed by Western Union, on duty until 10:00 p.m. every other night. March 1909. *Lewis Hine, National Child Labor Committee. Library of Congress.*

operators could not perform their duties for more than six hours straight without endangering their health.

Often working twelve to sixteen hours at a time, workers demanded an eight-hour day. They also pushed for overtime pay on Sundays and a 15 percent raise for every pay grade to help restore the losses they had been incurring since 1875.

One of the workers' demands was quite unusual for the time. The telegraphers' union insisted that all workers be paid based on their skill level, not their gender. Women as well as men worked as telegraph operators, took shorthand and dealt with the public. Women had even run military telegraph offices during the Civil War.

The Brotherhood of Telegraphers of the United States and Canada made equal pay for equal work one of its primary demands (even if its name didn't live up to its aspirations). The union was formed about two years before the 1883 strike, when several regional groups came together to form a united organization under the banner of the Knights of Labor. As a Knights affiliate, it accepted women as operators.

One male Hartford operator made the unions' demand clear. He told a newspaper reporter that "the clause demanding equal pay for equal work, whether done by men or women, was inserted in the bill of grievances from a sense of justice to the lady operators, who are as much overworked and unpaid in their departments as men." The striker explained that despite the equal effort and skill, women only received half of what men earned, from twenty-five to fifty dollars a month, compared to sixty to ninety dollars earned by male operators. (House painters and garment cutters earned twice as much as telegraphers.)

A local newspaper agreed with the strikers: "the 'woman question' is one that will longest engage the public attention. Equal pay for equal service is a just principle."

Union leaders met with Thomas T. Eckert, the general manager of Western Union, who rejected all their demands in a manner the unionists labeled "arrogant and disrespectful." They should not have been surprised. Eckert was an officer during the Civil War in charge of communications who passed critical information to Jay Gould just before a Union army victory or defeat. If the North was about to lose a battle, Eckert would wire Gould, and the robber baron would buy gold. If the North was about to win, Gould would switch to dollars. Once, during the Battle of Gettysburg, Eckert failed to pass along the inside information. Gould was furious.

Ironically, when Eckert got his job at Western Union, he issued a sixty-five-page list of rules and regulations to all operators. Rule no. 128 read, "All messages whatsoever including press reports, are strictly private and confidential, and must be treated thus by employees of the Company."

Ultimately, Eckert's reputation sank lower. On the day he had tickets to Ford's Theatre, Abraham Lincoln asked his secretary of war, Edward Stanton, to assign Eckert to the presidential security detail. Stanton refused, saying he had other work for Eckert to do. Lincoln then asked Eckert personally. Eckert refused. He spent that fateful night at home.

The Hartford strike began promptly at 12:05 on Thursday, July 19, 1883. One operator was in the middle of sending a dispatch when his co-workers walked out; he left with the message unfinished. Twelve of the thirteen Western Union operators walked out, leaving only the manager and chief operator. Both American Rapid operators struck as well, as did the lone worker at Mutual.

The linemen at the three companies "dropped their repairing instruments and retired from duty," according to a press report. Railroad and press operators were all told to stay on the job. This meant that the primary impact was on personal correspondence. But a Hartford newspaper reported that "public opinion here generally seems to sustain the operators in their movement." The operators who kept working "pledged themselves not to interfere in any way with the regular operators' strike."

For the first week, everyone coped. The public stopped coming to the telegraph offices and used the mail instead, since delivery and accuracy was no longer assured. One story circulated about three Hartford men visiting New Jersey who wired on a Saturday that they were coming home. When they arrived in the city on Monday, the telegram still had not been delivered.

In the meantime, groups of citizens mingled with the strikers at the intersection of Central Row and Main Street to discuss the latest news. The Hartford Knights of Labor office opened its doors so the strikers could meet. When not doing union business, strikers played baseball on a makeshift field in the North Meadows. The Western Union operators faced a team composed of employees from the other two companies for a seven-inning game. The united team won by a score of 15–9.

There was plenty of union work to do, as well. In order to ensure the local success of the strike, workers had to persuade out-of-town strikebreakers to stay away, such as one female Western Union operator who came into town from a rural office. Approached by the strikers, she listened to their arguments, signed a union card and returned home. Two operators who had traveled from White River Junction in Vermont were similarly initiated into the union by local operators. Two more from Burnside were discouraged from taking jobs as scabs. Samuel Adams, a New York lineman sent to American Rapid's Hartford office, was also met by strikers. He signed up and left for New York on the noon train.

Within six days, the American Rapid Company settled with the union, agreeing to 10 percent wage increases, "eight hours for a day's work," overtime pay for hours worked in excess of eight and Sunday overtime. The issue of pay equity was not directly addressed in the settlement. The company also agreed to hire strikers from other companies. But American Rapid was not the biggest target, and the strike against Western Union continued.

On August 8, several thousand union members and their families celebrated the American Rapid victory at their annual Union Grove picnic on Wethersfield Avenue. The event, which lasted until midnight, featured Samuel Gompers, the cigar maker who would soon become the first president of the American Federation of Labor.

The strike raised a fundamental question about ownership of a business that was crucial to the national interest. Leading newspapers, including those in New Haven, Bridgeport and Norwich, lobbied for a telegraph system that was regulated just like the post office. One local editorial writer summed up the public sentiment: "'Let the government take the telegraph' is the universal demand."

Cracks in operators' solidarity appeared in other parts of the country. There were reports that some operators who were allowed to stay on the job were doing the work of strikers. In Boston and New York, some strikers returned to work. Desperate acts of sabotage of telegraph lines occurred outside of New York City, and there were sporadic attacks on scabs. In Hartford, signs were posted on Western Union poles offering a $500 reward for information that would lead to the conviction of anyone damaging company property. "It is not likely that a single reward will ever come to Hartford," a local paper wrote.

National union leaders tried to meet with Eckert in New York on August 15 during a meeting of the Western Union executive committee, but he refused. The Western Union strike was called off on August 17. Some Hartford strikers were rehired and forced to sign "yellow dog contracts" requiring them to never join a union. Others, like lineman Walter Clark and a depot office worker identified as Miss Lester, were not reinstated. It is reasonable to presume that they were blacklisted, a common tactic to thwart future union efforts.

A local newspaper blamed the workers' situation on the union and described it as an "organization which can get its members into trouble but cannot pull them through." In a way, this conservative viewpoint was correct. By deciding which of the operators would strike and which would stay on the job, the union weakened its bargaining position. Jay Gould could be beaten in only one way: by a strong united front.

9
FASCISM IN FASHION

Benito Mussolini rose to power in Italy in the 1920s and is credited with developing modern-day fascism. For many, the ideology did not carry a negative connotation at first, since neither he nor Adolph Hitler had shown their true, monstrous intentions.

In time, the world came to know the brutality of fascism: the absolute state, the expansion of empire by conquest, the creation of scapegoats used to ratchet up popular fear, the sexist mindset that glamorized machismo and war and the anti-intellectual culture dismissive of human rights.

The definition of fascism would seem to contradict the tenets of Yankee independence and American democracy. Yet more than a few Hartford residents admired Mussolini for the image he projected: his jutting jaw, his hands chopping the air and his testosterone-fueled attitude. Il Duce ("the Leader," as Mussolini named himself), promised to make Italy great again, which spoke to many immigrants who longed for their homeland.

Mussolini's imperial ambitions struck a chord with a range of people. The famous Hartford poet Wallace Stevens admired the strongman image the dictator created for himself ("I am pro-Mussolini personally" he wrote in a letter to his publisher).

An executive from the Manufacturers Association of Connecticut visited the fascist regime and returned with great praise for its revitalized economic system. Italian Americans marched through the streets of Hartford when Ethiopia surrendered to Mussolini's invasion.

Father Kelly's Fascist Gold

Father Andrew J. Kelly was a big Mussolini booster. He was also the pastor of St. Anthony's Church in Hartford's Italian east end. Kelly found fertile ground for his pro-fascist stance among many (but not all) of his two thousand parishioners.

In 1936, Mussolini put out a call to Italian women to donate their gold wedding rings to the government in a show of loyalty and sacrifice. In exchange, he offered them iron bands, symbols of Italian strength. "Gold and Country" was engraved on the inside of each ring.

Father Kelly convinced five hundred Hartford women to give up their gold bands at a blessing ceremony on Sunday, May 24, 1936. "The substitution of iron for gold wedding rings by Italian wives," the priest said, "symbolizes… the unanimity of Italian sentiment in favor of its government." One hundred

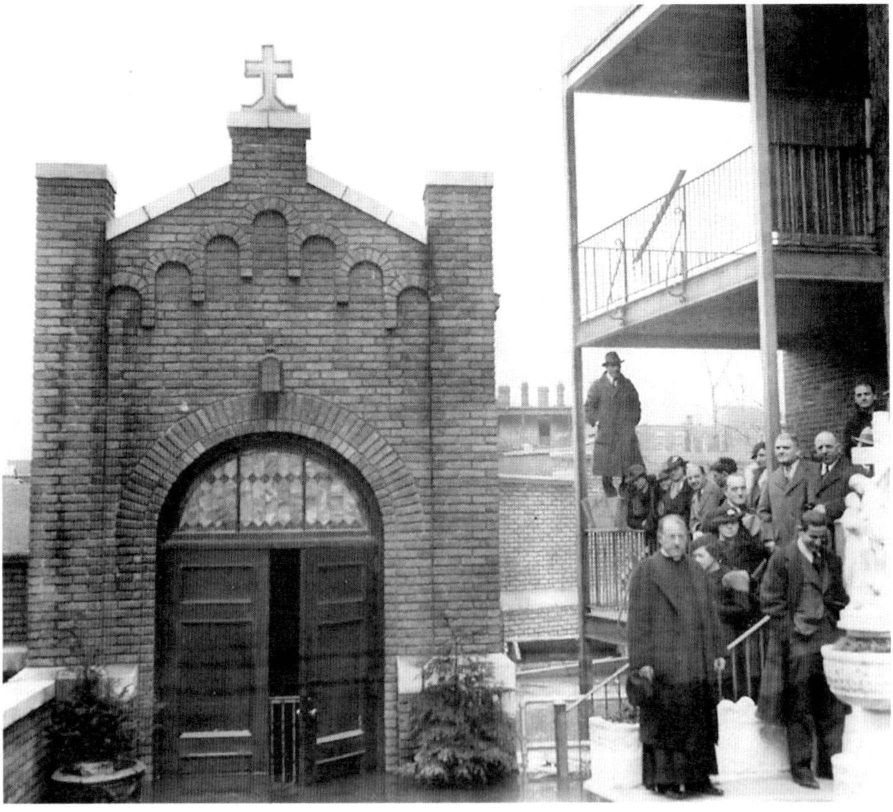

Father Andrew J. Kelly with parishioners at St. Anthony's Church on Hartford's east side. *Courtesy of Dennis F. Sullivan.*

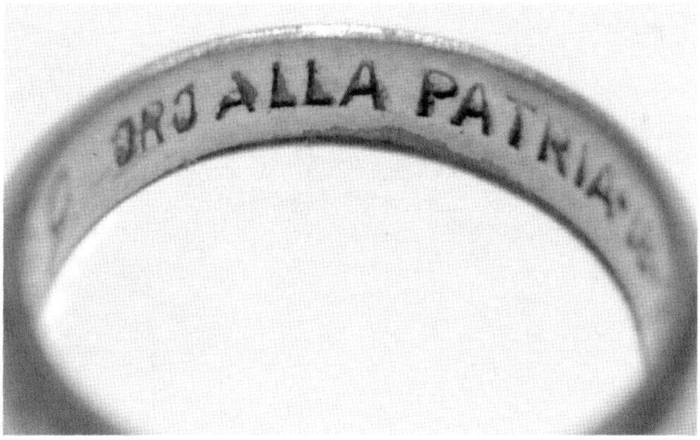

From Mussolini with love: Father Kelly distributed 455 iron rings from Il Duce to Hartford women in exchange for their gold wedding bands. *Author's collection.*

rings were also distributed to women of the Hartford Italian Congregational Church, and as many as one thousand iron bands were delivered to Catholic women in New Britain.

The pastor also formed a "Boys' Brigade" at Saint Anthony's, patterned after the Boy Scouts but a tad more militaristic. The youngsters were "cadets" formed into "brigades" and "battalions." The adult leaders were officers in the Connecticut National Guard. The boys were praised by Kelly for their discipline.

Father Kelly was an outspoken and controversial figure. He lashed out at birth control advocates, including Katharine Houghton Hepburn, labeling them "busybody humanitarians" who promoted coercive and "satanic" practices by spreading "cancerous doctrines" like family planning.

Kelly was a supporter of Charles E. Coughlin, the anti-Semitic, pro-Nazi "radio priest." Coughlin had a huge listening audience and was influential in American politics. (Kelly dabbled in radio, as well.) His National Union for Social Justice was a million-member political action organization. Coughlin also promoted the Christian Front, a paramilitary group that used vigilantism against agents of "Jewish communism."

Hartford had local versions of both of these organizations. Locally, the National Union was led by Henry White, an employee of the Terry Steam Turbine company. The Christian Front in Hartford dissolved by 1940, when the FBI raided the New York chapter and arrested eighteen members who were planning to assassinate public figures.

LOCAL OPPONENTS OF A BRUTAL REGIME

There were vocal critics of fascist ideology, certainly. On October 27, 1936, *It Can't Happen Here* was performed by the Federal Theater Project, one of the New Deal's progressive jobs programs. The Nobel Prize winner Sinclair Lewis had refashioned his dystopian story into a dramatic play. It opened simultaneously in twenty-one cities in eighteen states, including Hartford and Bridgeport. Lewis's work was performed just five months after Father Kelly collected the gold wedding rings for Mussolini.

The play was largely set in New England. A quote attributed to Lewis describes the danger he wanted to capture: "When fascism comes to America, it will be wrapped in the flag and carrying a cross." His characters were all homegrown Americans, representing both the left and right in American politics. As he wrote in his novel, "In America the struggle was befogged by the fact that the worst Fascists were they who disowned the word 'Fascism' and preached enslavement to Capitalism under the style of Constitutional and Traditional Native American Liberty."

The author of *Main Street* and *Babbitt* believed that the real dangers lay not in an outside invasion but in the cynical use of patriotism and Christianity. Lewis could have been speaking about Father Andrew Kelly.

While certain Hartford clergy were seduced by Il Duce, others spoke out forcefully. Rabbi Abraham J. Feldman was a popular orator and the head of Connecticut's first synagogue, Temple Beth Israel. On the celebration of Connecticut's 300th birthday, he gave a clear warning before an audience of hundreds of Christians and Jews:

> *The propertied classes, in fear of socialism or any left-wing movement, are tempted to turn to Fascism because Fascism recognizes property rights and the profit motive. They look hopefully towards Fascism and are willing to play with it and barter away our hard won American ideals. And yet, in my judgement, they are stupidly oblivious to the fact that under Fascism property rights are greatly curtailed because they are completely subordinated to the will of the state and the ruling group.*

HUCK FINN AND SPANISH WAR VICTIMS

On October 11, 1938, a crowd gathered on the Old State House lawn as artist Alton Tobey set up his easel. Insurance company workers on their lunch break watched the painter and his three colleagues as they worked on large posters depicting the fight against fascism in Spain.

Tobey's talents were focused on the state of the world, dominated by the rise of Hitler, Mussolini and Franco in Spain. The painter had been recruited to create a mural by Jerome Stavola, an art instructor at the Hartford Federal College (another New Deal program). Along with Bob Beebe and Joseph Scarozzo, they were preparing for a major event at Bushnell Memorial Hall to raise funds for a relief ship that would soon leave New York Harbor. It was headed for the beleaguered population of Spain in a desperate fight for life against allied fascist forces.

After a decade of dictatorship, Spanish workers and peasants had, in 1931, elected a progressive government that instituted land reform and the eight-hour day. In response, the country's right wing gathered allies within the army and the Catholic Church and gained critical backing from the fascist leaders of Germany and Italy.

Just before being called on to publicize the Bushnell fundraiser, Alton Tobey had been busy completing a mural at the Hartford Public Library's Campfield Branch in the city's south end. For his subjects, the young artist used the literature of Mark Twain and Harriet Beecher Stowe.

Characters from *A Connecticut Yankee in King Arthur's Court* mingled with those of *Uncle Tom's Cabin*. Huck Finn, Tom Sawyer, Simon Legree and Eliza all inhabited the library's façade. These novels, written by two authors who called Hartford home, provided sharp commentary on the social injustices of their time.

Now Tobey put his skill to work to protest injustice in Spain, using art to help shape the debate over defending the Spanish Republic. He had likely been influenced by *Guernica*, a painting that depicts the 1937 destruction of a Basque town by German warplanes. Guernica was firebombed by Hitler's Condor Legion and one thousand civilians died, many of them by machine-gun fire from the air as they fled. That same year, Pablo Picasso turned this war crime into his masterpiece of outrage and pain.

As the crowd at the Old State House grew, so did the dissatisfaction by some onlookers over the political content of the murals. Some thought it was communistic; others thought it might be pro-Nazi.

Tobey was putting the finishing touches on the scene of a child in a German military uniform when an Officer Dooley, who had been directing traffic on Main Street, walked over to the painter to see what the commotion was all about. Instead of allowing the artists to finish, or at least explain what they were doing, the Hartford cop ordered them to stop.

The painting was interrupted that day, but the artists' work continued. Tobey's colleague Jerome Stavola was soon named to a statewide committee of Italian Americans who organized protests against Mussolini's treatment of Jews in Italy.

At Bushnell Hall, hundreds of local supporters dug into their pockets to help buy food and medicine for the relief efforts while they listened to the Spanish ambassador plead for the fate of his people.

None of the efforts by Hartford people could stop the rise of fascism in Europe, let alone the next world war. Patriotic Hartfordites joined the armed forces and did their part for the war effort. But Father Kelly and his fellow sympathizers had demonstrated a viral strain in American history, one that mutates to fit the times.

10

HELL HOLE

Seyms Street Jail

For more than a century, the Seyms Street jail housed the criminal, the innocent and the notorious. At one time or another, civil rights protesters, antiwar activists and Black Panthers all found themselves incarcerated there. Despite reformers' attempts to improve the inhumane conditions, prisoners suffered.

The notoriety of this Hartford jail, commonly known by its location instead of its name, exposed the truth behind the "progressive" U.S. criminal justice system; it even gained national condemnation in 1920 from a future Supreme Court judge. Built in 1873 for 350 prisoners, the Hartford County jail sometimes held as many as 600 men and women in the summer months. There was no sewage line; for a century, inmates had to empty their own waste buckets. Medical care was almost nonexistent; prisoners might leave Seyms Street sicker than when they went in. Communicable diseases then became an even greater health hazard to the public.

At least seventy-five men escaped from Seyms Street over the years. The first was George Brewer in 1894. He fled on his horse, Jeff, to New Jersey. Others actually sawed through iron bars to escape. Some strolled away from work crews.

Some seized the moment, without much planning. In 1977, Howard Landry took off barefoot in his prison clothes. He was captured on the Route 84 highway.

Archie Ferguson may have been the only man to break *into* the jail. At Christmastime in 1946, he threw a stone through a restaurant window so the police would take him to Seyms Street for shelter.

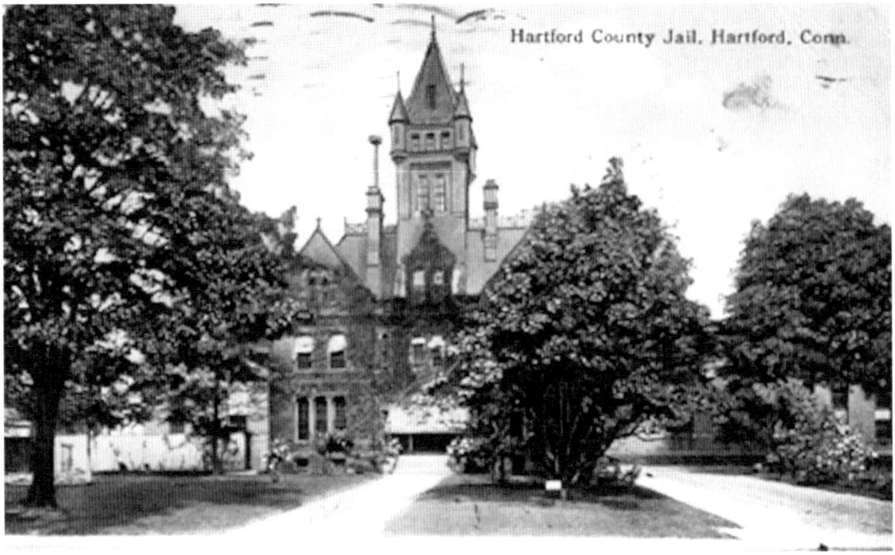

Seyms Street Jail, idealized in a picture postcard. *Hartford History Center*.

Most of Seyms Street's history is not amusing, however. When the 1919–20 Palmer Raids swept through Connecticut and the nation, one hundred men were held for months at Seyms Street. Attorney General A. Mitchell Palmer led a nationwide roundup of immigrant workers, union organizers and suspected radicals on flimsy excuses. Those held prisoner were denied basic rights, including not being charged with a specific crime or offered bail. Some were eventually freed; many of the foreign-born were deported. Union efforts were crippled by Palmer's actions, and families were torn apart.

The *Nation* magazine helped lead the fight against the nationwide mass jailings. In addition to popular protest against the incarcerations, a committee of well-known, highly respected lawyers investigated Palmer's massive civil rights violations. One of those jurists was Felix Frankfurter of Massachusetts, later appointed to the Supreme Court by Franklin Roosevelt.

The first example in the magazine's May 1920 report exposed conditions at Seyms Street. It criticized the use of four particular cells—called punishment rooms—that held political prisoners (those thought to be anarchists, communists or members of the Industrial Workers of the World). The cells were located directly over the jail's boiler room. The cell floor was often so hot that an inmate's hands or feet would burn. There were no windows and no light bulbs.

Prisoners held in punishment rooms received one glass of water and a slice of bread every twelve hours. By any reasonable definition, the conditions amounted to torture.

Despite the bad publicity, nothing changed. A Connecticut legislative committee "sharply criticized" the jail in 1938 for its "medieval punishment cells."

STRIKE!

In 1967, 145 inmates at Hartford's Seyms Street jail organized a nonviolent sit-down strike. Instead of returning to their cells for the night, they demanded to negotiate with the warden. They were fed up with the poor treatment and living conditions in the facility they knew as the "hell hole."

At 10:00 p.m. on August 9, the inmates, all from the maximum security ward, took their stand. Among the twenty demands they delivered to the authorities were complaints of overcrowding, poor food, insufficient medical care and abuse by guards. Authorities called out the Hartford police, who surrounded the jail. The state police were put on alert. The warden rushed in from his home.

The prisoners eventually negotiated with a committee of prison officials, a state senator and a newspaper reporter on these and other issues, including lack of access to bail bondsmen and their own legal documents, restricted visitor privileges, jail job segregation and lack of exercise opportunity (five hundred men lived in the building at the time). They were allowed one shower a week with no way to buy toilet paper, towels, soap or toothbrushes. There was no running water in the cells. Sometimes, they got no water from the guards. Lice, roaches and rats moved about undisturbed.

Solitary confinement could be made indefinite at the whim of a correction officer, the inmates said. They were stripped naked when they entered solitary and had to urinate and defecate on the floor because there were no toilets, not even buckets.

Four years after the Seyms Street strike, the Attica prison uprising in September 1971 became the most well-known jail rebellion in U.S. history. Refusal by New York governor Nelson Rockefeller to meet directly with inmates over their grievances—many like those of the Seyms Street strikers—led to an armed raid by authorities. Ten hostages and twenty-six inmates were killed. After much criticism and a (still secret) government report, the State of New York paid $8 million to inmates and their families to settle a lawsuit.

At Seyms Street, the negotiations halted for the night. After they were guaranteed no reprisals, the inmates ended their strike at around 2:30 in the morning. The next day, state officials toured the facility. Some called the conditions "appalling" as they viewed soiled mattresses and smelled the unwashed inmates.

They met David Bradshaw, twenty-two years old and already a civil rights veteran from his voter registration efforts in the South. Bradshaw said he was picked up during the recent disturbances in Hartford's north end. When he arrived at Seyms Street, he was immediately placed in "Siberia," a section of the jail worse than the rest. Jail authorities promised some immediate improvements. They insisted that other changes could only be made with more state funding.

In 1971, state lawmakers Leonard Frazier and Wilber Smith nailed a placard to the jail door with the words "Unfit for Human Occupancy" as part of their protest against Seyms Street conditions. Local college students held a rally the same year to bring attention to the worsening conditions. Inmates filed a class-action lawsuit in 1974 charging cruel and unusual punishment.

In 1976, the Committee Against Police Repression led 150 people in a march to Seyms Street. It had been the target of public criticism since 1920, but little had changed. The jail continued to be the site of protests by local community activists and college students who demanded reforms to the jail's "sub-human" conditions, in the words of a former corrections official.

The Connecticut General Assembly authorized funds to build a new jail in 1966. For ten years, the state fought with suburban officials, who all rejected a facility in their towns before Hartford was once again chosen as the building site. Seyms Street finally closed, and prisoners were transferred to the new Hartford Correctional Center on Weston Street—still in the city's north end—on July 6, 1977. Just one month earlier, two men had committed suicide in their cells.

11

FALES & GRAY CATASTROPHE

Not Just an Accident

John McCuen's arm was found some distance from his body. McCuen was the engineer at the Fales & Gray Car Works in Hartford. On Friday, March 3, 1854, the steam boiler he was attending to exploded, killing him and eighteen other workers and seriously injuring twenty-three more.

After an inquiry that lasted six days, it was determined that McCuen's carelessness was the cause of the massive explosion. There were intimations that McCuen had been drinking on the job.

Hartford was ill prepared to care for the dozens of workers injured in the blast. After the inquest concluded and donations were collected for the grieving families, the city fathers decided a hospital must be built. The cornerstone for Hartford Hospital was laid in 1857.

More to the Story

The hospital's creation was not the end of the story, although that's what history books would have us believe. One brave voice spoke out to challenge the accepted narrative of a single careless man responsible for the wreckage. The Reverend Frederic Hinckley of the Unitarian Church of the Savior addressed his congregation on March 12 after the results of the inquiry were reported. He told his audience:

> *Where are those fathers, husbands, men—your brothers and mine? Shall we answer the question—answer it in a word? Sacrificed. Yes, sacrificed to the reckless spirit of enterprise of this mid-century; uselessly, murderously destroyed that more physical power might be obtained, more speed secured, more work performed, and greater materials produced.*
>
> *The immediate cause of the explosion itself was doubtless the momentary carelessness of the engineer and dearly did he pay for his neglect. But in this, as in most other instances, that cause did not stand alone. It was connected with others.*
>
> [Speeding up the boiler] *is acknowledged to be unsafe...in the estimate of some who ought to be qualified to judge, beyond its proper limits.*
>
> [The operator] *is not alone responsible. Some portion of that responsibility must fall back upon the spirit pervading the establishment and fostered by it.*

"The truth is," Reverend Hinckley continued, "it is a fearful power, whether productive or destructive in its operation. Man must deal with it wisely and cautiously or he finds himself powerless before it."

Hinckley made it clear that his sermon was not meant to accuse the owners "for the purpose of dragging them personally before the bar of popular judgement." The firm was no different from any other company that was part of the "reckless enterprise of the times," he believed.

The minister laid out what was lacking at Fales & Gray before the explosion. The steam power "should be entrusted only to thoroughly qualified and efficient men," he explained. It was not enough that a man understood the workings of the machine, as the owners had testified. Such a man had to understand the science behind steam power and must have the qualities of "sobriety, promptness, and decision." Next, Hinckley observed, the boiler should have been located in an area that "shall cause the least possible destruction in case of accident." The company did not "have any right to thus endanger the lives of his fellows."

"Life, practical, busy life is thus turned into a race between power and speed on the one hand, and human safety and human existence on the other," he said. "How often, alas, the safety and the existence find themselves outstripped in the race." The grand jury agreed. Its report cited the proximity of the steam boiler as a major cause of workers' deaths.

Reverend Hinckley took a beating in the press for presuming to speak on industrial matters. He was warned, in essence, to stick to his congregation's spiritual lives and leave the welfare of workers to the businessmen.

The reverend's words were prescient. As the author Jack London wrote some years later, "Let us not destroy those wonderful machines that produce efficiently and cheaply. Let us control them. Let us profit by their efficiency and cheapness. Let us run them for ourselves."

Frederic Hinckley's warnings, however, were not heeded. In 1898, thirty years after the Fales & Gray disaster, the *Machinists' Journal* wrote: "A carnival of carnage that takes place every day, month and year in the realm of industry, the thousands of useful lives that are annually sacrificed to the Moloch of greed, the blood tribute paid by labor to capitalism, brings forth no shout of vengeance and reparation....Death comes in thousands of instances in mill and mine, claims his victims, and no popular uproar is heard."

WORKERS DID NOT COUNT

There was a massive increase in workplace deaths from the 1850s into the twentieth century. Marc Linder, an author and labor statistician, wrote that "in the nineteenth century, what counted was what was counted." In other words, if we didn't know the full extent of who was injured or killed on the job, it just didn't matter. We do know, however, that there were two thousand steam boiler explosions between 1880 and 1890.

There were no numbers kept on all U.S. workplace accidents until individual states began the process in the 1880s. Even then, it would take the 1970 OSHA (Occupational Safety and Health Act) to require a nationwide collection of statistics. OSHA also began to introduce federal workplace protections and enforcement laws.

In contrast, England and Germany had begun to pass workplace safety laws as early as 1844, a decade before the Fales & Gray explosion. Those countries required governments to annually record industrial deaths and accidents. In addition, they began to demand safety guards for dangerous machinery.

In 1912, Dr. Allan D. Risteen of Traveler's Insurance Company reported to a Hartford audience on national safety numbers. "Figures show that 100 men are killed every day as a result of industrial accidents," he declared. "Two million a year are merely injured." Risteen started collecting figures on steam boiler explosions in 1892. He compared the figures with those of England and Germany. "I have found that ten in this country die to one in England and twenty-seven to one in Germany." Risteen believed that industrial managers were "too conservative," refusing to spend money to prevent accidents.

E. Sidney Berry agreed. After Risteen's speech, Berry was moved to conclude that "this is a great country for liberty, but we lay more emphasis on liberty of property than we do on liberty of life." Berry was the lawyer for the Hartford Steam Boiler Inspection & Insurance Company.

12

HARTFORD'S ORIGINAL SIN

The first recorded murder victim in Hartford was Louis Berbice in 1639. He was the slave of Gysbert Opdyck, the influential leader of the Dutch fort, known as the House of Hope, near the Connecticut River. The Opdyck genealogy records the incident:

> *Gysbert Opdyck...declares that Lewis Barbese* [sic] *took a pan to bake cookies and as the fire was too hot for the boy, Opdyck took the pan from him and ordered him to bring a shovel. The shovel which the boy brought was dirty, whereupon Opdyck whipped the boy who, to escape the whipping, ran away and Opdyck gave him a kick in the side. The boy ran before the door where he fell down. Opdyck went toward the boy and found a crooked knife bent like a hook and that the boy had a wound "left side near his arm wherefrom he died very soon."*

Later, Opdyck would say it was an accident. He was never found guilty of any crime. Call it Hartford's Original Sin.

Was our form of bondage kinder and gentler than slavery in the South? As Hartford's Harriet Beecher Stowe wrote, "The north wanted all the benefits of slavery without the screams and horrors."

Over the centuries, we have tried to make it so. That's one reason why much has been written about the "Negro Governors," an early Connecticut practice in which a male slave was chosen to serve as the "leader" of all the state's enslaved people. Almost without exception, this phenomenon

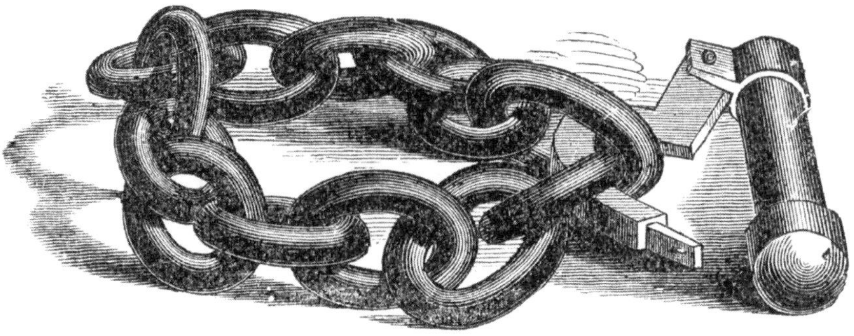

Chains used to bind an enslaved person. *Interfoto/Alamy stock photo.*

has been considered a harmless, almost progressive feature of slavery in eighteenth- and nineteenth-century New England. Orville Platt, whose work is often cited on the subject, called it "a curious habit that negroes fell into."

The subtle implication is that this "government" was a positive aspect of the chattel slavery system. "We were studying a lot of things on slavery that was all depressing and about getting whipped. Finally, we found some uplifting experience like a black governor," concluded one African American middle school student whose Hartford class tackled the subject in 1998. But just how benign was this episode of our state's history?

The custom probably began in the 1750s in Connecticut and spread to other New England colonies (and later, states). It continued into the 1840s. How the practice began is not precisely known, but the annual event was likely used to ensure that slaveholders could keep an eye on their property.

One day each year, white male citizens traveled to Hartford to tally votes for the state's gubernatorial election. (There were one-year terms until 1875.) Slaves would likewise hold a celebration in honor of their new "Governor." (In other venues, he was called the "King.") The festival included an elaborate parade down Main Street led by the Negro Governor in military regalia. The event always concluded with a huge party and plenty of food and alcohol provided by the slave owner, ending in a "drunken riot," according to one account.

THE "CURIOUS HABIT THAT NEGROES FELL INTO"

Some historians have theorized that by having their own "leader," African Americans were being introduced to the experience of eventual citizenship. The Negro Governor election has been described as "a custom to give the negro an opportunity to become a politician." The "Negro Elections" were "preserved for victories yet to come," writes one academic, as if either blacks or whites could have anticipated post–Civil War emancipation.

Still others have speculated that slaves considered the event a continuation of the self-governance they had practiced in their homelands (although generations had passed, and some African tribes were led by women). In any case, the "election" was controlled by the slave masters: an outgoing governor appointed his successor with the owner's approval. Having one's own slave as governor was a status symbol for the white master, giving him "bragging rights," if you will, and arguably a personal means of influence over the slave population. The governor appointed deputies for largely ceremonial positions.

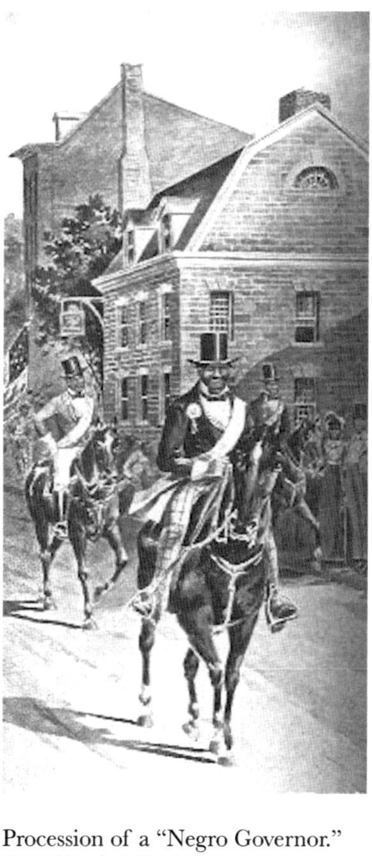

Procession of a "Negro Governor." *From Hartford-HWP.*

His real job was to serve as judge and jury for any slave who committed an infraction, as defined by white law or custom. As punishment, the governor could confiscate a slave's property, if he had any, or sometimes have the offender flogged. In an 1851 history published by the *Hartford Courant,* one particular Negro Governor "unmercifully" meted out punishment. He was described as "a terror to the blacks, and kept them orderly." The writer left no doubt that the practice was successful, concluding, "we have got a well-behaved set of them now, taken as a whole."

Even after there were no slaves living in Connecticut (the local census stopped counting slaves in 1840), blacks could not vote in the state's real elections. African

Americans were formally disenfranchised by the general assembly in 1818; it is unlikely that any free black men voted even before that time. Instead, they had to be satisfied with the sham Negro Governor practice.

Social Control

Far from being a harmless event, the Negro Governor election acted as a form of social control: it showed every slave the consequences of disobedience. And because one of their own was given permission to inflict corporal punishment, it kept the white masters' hands clean. As one writer euphemistically put it, the practice was "a means of the well-ordering of the negro population."

"[These] punishments were carried out by the Negro executioner after the culprit had first been sentenced by a white magistrate," according to Dr. Lorenzo Johnston Greene. "This was the case of a Connecticut thief whose sentence of thirty lashes was publicly administered by 'Squire Nep,' a Negro barber, on the town green."

"Negro 'government,'" argued Greene, "induced the slaves to inform on and to punish their fellows [so that] the threat to the masters' security was diminished." The Negro Governor charade "served as a subtle means of slave control," Greene wrote.

"Those slaves who were the object of especially kind treatment by their owners manifested their gratitude even to the extent of giving their lives in protection of their masters' children," Greene said. Despite this amiable New England conceit, "there were Negroes who found their bondage so intolerable that they committed suicide." (Lorenzo Greene was an African American historian, civil rights activist and labor advocate, born in Ansonia in 1899.) There was a good reason to maintain this form of control. Over the years, graphic details of slave revolts were widely reported in Connecticut newspapers. Even if African Americans did not read these accounts, their masters surely did.

There were slave insurrections in Hartford (1657) and New London (1768), as well as in Boston and numerous other Massachusetts towns. In 1776, the *Connecticut Courant* warned its readers to "Remember the bribing of negro slaves to assassinate their masters."

Rebellions outside of New England by enslaved men and women dated back at least to 1739 with the Stono Revolt in Florida. In 1741, a series of suspicious fires in New York led nervous whites to believe a slave uprising was imminent. Rebellions led by Gabriel Prosser (1800) and Denmark Vesey (1822) added to the slaveholders' fears. In 1831, Nat Turner led eighty followers in deadly attacks on whites in Virginia. It was in all the Hartford papers.

THOSE IN POWER WRITE THE HISTORY

To investigate the truth behind the Negro Governors is to face an enormous hurdle: all the firsthand accounts were written by white people. Every essay, newspaper article and lecture, and every subsequent study, were framed by whites' own personal interests and views on slavery. Every subsequent treatment is based on these earliest accounts. Is this because slaves couldn't write their own history? It is true that, in many states, slaves who were literate were prosecuted as criminals.

In fact, there are many powerful written works by African Americans, both slave and free. Hartford's Reverend Hosea Easton wrote his widely read treatise on the condition of black people in 1837. Reverend James Pennington of Hartford wrote *The Origin and History of the Colored People* (1841), the first history of its kind, and then his autobiography, *The Fugitive Blacksmith* (1849).

Phyllis Wheatley's poetry (1773) spoke eloquently of her desire for freedom. David Walker's "Appeal to the Colored Citizens of the World" (1829) was a militant cry for rebellion. The autobiography of Frederick Douglass (1845) recounted his years in slavery and ultimate liberation. None of these works included a defense of the Negro Governor phenomenon.

TORTURE: BREAKING THE WILL OF A COMMUNITY

There is evidence that in Hartford, the Negro Governor, as directed by his white owner, engaged in brutality beyond imposing fines or the occasional lashing. In one of the oldest descriptions of the governor's punitive power, there is a very brief mention of the use of *bastinado*. This archaic term denotes a form of torture.

Unlike flogging, bastinado entails the beating of a victim's feet (and sometimes hands or hips) as a punishment. In one definition, it "relies on the fact that the foot is a fragile appendage with many bones, tendons, joints and muscles. It is also a place where nerve endings are close to the surface and therefore particularly susceptible to pain." The physical effects, besides the immediate pain, can involve permanent deformity and chronic disability, including muscle necrosis (tissue death). Bastinado has been used for hundreds of years around the world to elicit cooperation from torture victims.

Why would white slaveholders grant the power of physical torture to the Negro Governor? As the group Physicians for Human Rights reports, the aim of torture is to "dehumanize the victim, break his/her will, and at the same time, set horrific examples for those who come in contact with the victim. In this way *torture can break or damage the will and coherence of entire communities*" (emphasis added). Torture has always been social control at its most base level.

SANITIZING HISTORY

Also troubling is the fact that as the Negro Governor story has been passed down through generations, each iteration has been further sanitized. Early accounts were full of racist terminology, written in a highly patronizing manner and contemptuous of blacks who participated in Election Day activities. There was no outrage at the use of violence against slaves, however. After all, they were property to be bought and sold.

Even on the rare occasion in which a writer consulted former slaves to record their recollections, there is no assurance of their accuracy, and no guarantee the stories were not sugarcoated for the benefit of the white interviewer, telling him what he wanted to hear. Yet today, we are informed that "the black community in Connecticut had its own parallel government during the colonial and early American period," according to one recent newspaper feature. Consciously or not, the Negro Governor myth diminishes Hartford's real complicity in the practice of slavery.

FREDERICK DOUGLASS, UNWELCOME IN HARTFORD

There was plenty of support for abolitionism in Hartford, yet young Frederick Douglass did not find his first trip to the city welcoming. He and his comrades "found several towns in which people closed their doors and refused to entertain the subject," he wrote in his autobiography *Life and Times*.

"Notably among these were Hartford, Conn., and Grafton Mass. In the former [we] determined to hold our meetings under the open sky, which we did in a little court under the eaves of the 'sanctuary' ministered unto by the Rev. Dr. [Joel] Hawes, with much satisfaction to ourselves and I think great advantage to our cause." The site of this speech was the First Church of Christ in Hartford.

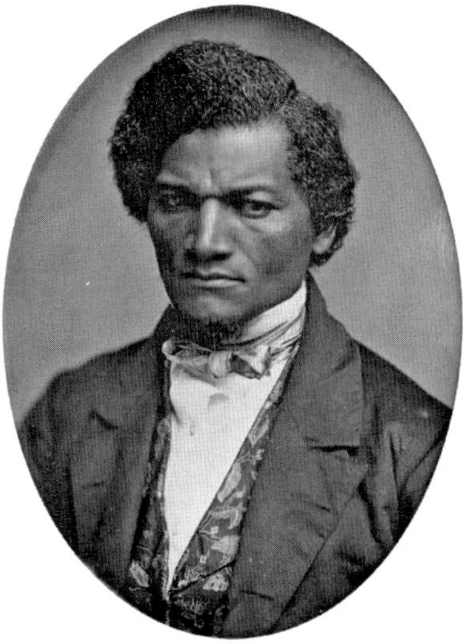

Frederick Douglass, around 1843. The abolitionist was twenty-three at the time he first spoke in Hartford. *Daguerreotype by Samuel J. Miller.*

As time went on and the pro- and antislavery debate sharpened, Frederick Douglass gained greater popularity. In October 1854, he was in Chicago to rebut the pro-slavery rhetoric of U.S. senator Stephen A. Douglas. An antislavery Hartford newspaper reported on the event, exclaiming, "the Black Douglass against the White one! Who can doubt as to the result!" The senator from Illinois, nicknamed "the little giant," would later debate Abraham Lincoln in 1858 and then lose the 1860 presidential election to Honest Abe.

The black freedom struggle in Connecticut did not end with the Civil War. In 1865, the state's voters overwhelmingly rejected giving African Americans the franchise. It is important to note that only white men could vote at the time. Just one town, Meriden, supported voting rights for black people in that referendum. Frederick Douglass went on to address the people of Meriden in 1868. Despite racist treatment by Stephen Ives, the landlord of the Meriden House, where Douglass stayed, the speech was well received.

Ironically, present-day Hartford has a memorial plaque commemorating a speech by Stephen Douglas at the corner of Main and Pearl Streets. A permanent memorial and garden was dedicated to Frederick Douglass in 2017. The "open sky" court under the First Church eaves, where Frederick Douglass first spoke in Hartford, has become a fitting place for such a long-delayed honor.

RIOTS: THE CITY BURNS

"No Danger of Race Riots in Hartford, Police Officials Say." It was August 4, 1919. Hartford's African American ministers feared that the white mob violence raging through dozens of U.S. cities could well take place in their own town. The city's black population was still small, but growing. Those who had escaped the segregated South found they still faced widespread discrimination in Hartford.

The ministers were reassured by police chief Garrett J. Farrell that "there was no likelihood of a dispute between white and colored residents." Reports of a racial incident on Windsor Street was probably "phoney," Farrell said, although, in fact, the area was frequently the scene of disputes between police and black men at illegal gambling clubs. Hartford's black clergy used their pulpits to condemn wanton attacks on black communities in what became known as "Red Summer." Even as their sermons were being heard, Chicago was in its sixth day of deadly rioting. The violence had begun when Eugene Williams, a seventeen-year-old black youth, was caught swimming outside the "colored only" part of Lake Michigan. Williams was stoned by whites on the beach; he was knocked unconscious and drowned. The Chicago police refused to make any arrests.

Young black men around the city lashed out at the Jim Crow justice, and white gangs answered in kind. In all, at least fifty Chicago residents, overwhelmingly black, were killed. Another five hundred were injured, and one thousand black families lost their homes to arson.

For Hartford's black leadership, the riots in Chicago and other northern cities were a premonition. The symptoms in Chicago were present in their own neighborhoods: substandard opportunities, de facto segregation and young people unwilling to tolerate racist attitudes. It would only be a matter of time.

A CENTURY OF WARNING SIGNS

Although Connecticut saw no widespread violence that summer, local African American leaders and social service advocates were exposing intolerable and persistent living conditions that, some warned, were eventually bound to spark uprisings.

Black families in Hartford lived in "the worst housing conditions in the country," according to a 1908 New York tenement commission. A special

Hartford mayoral housing investigation concurred and provided specific solutions, which were ignored.

Pastor W.B. Reed of the Colored Men's Civic League targeted racist exclusion from local labor unions as a major factor in keeping black workers in low-wage jobs. In 1918, he declared, "We are united to fight for a man's place in the field of industry." There was "practically universal prejudice" in Hartford against hiring black and foreign-born workers, according to the U.S. Employment Service. A federal spokesman pleaded with local employers in 1919 that these workers were "fairly good citizens" whose discontent would increase to the point that they would end up becoming Bolsheviks. Only two black workers found jobs in the region's defense industry, according to a 1941 public health study.

Child mortality was reported to be an astonishing 180 per 1,000 for black children, in contrast to 70 per 1,000 for whites, according to a 1923 Yale Medical School health survey. Throughout the 1930s, tuberculosis hit Connecticut's black families the hardest. The TB death rates among blacks were 182 per 1,000; white deaths were 35 per 1,000.

Every new report or investigation, and every prescription for change, received lukewarm responses from local government and business leaders. Every decade, the problems got worse.

SMALL STEPS

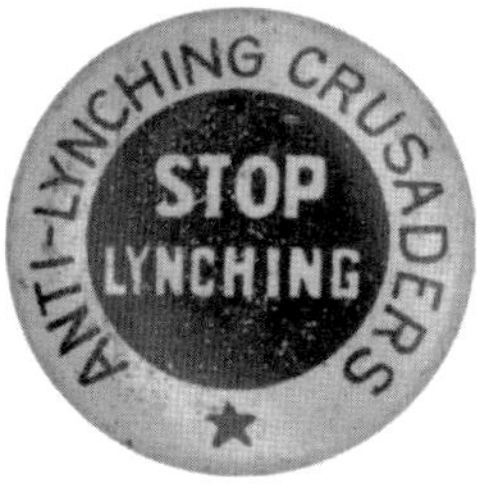

The Anti-Lynching Crusaders, a national group with state headquarters in Hartford. *Author's collection.*

For the first half of the twentieth century, Connecticut's black communities concentrated on the steady work of improvement and reform. Early civil rights pioneers fought entrenched attitudes and institutional bias in every aspect of their lives, with almost no help from local or state government.

Mary Townsend Seymour organized black female tobacco workers with no labor laws to protect them and scant labor support. Dr. P.H.C. Arms, a black physician, ran for mayor in 1906, but it took another fifty years for the first African American to win a city council seat.

The Reverend Walter Gay, pastor of Union Baptist Church, told the Hartford Equal Rights Club that the campaign for women's right to vote and the struggle for black civil rights were closely linked and should be taken up together.

Ethel Thompson sued a Hartford hotel in 1945 when she and her family were denied a room, but they lost because Judge Abraham Ribicoff ruled that there was not enough proof.

Mansfield Tilly and Warren Stewart, both skilled electricians and World War II veterans, had to fight building trade union opposition for five years until they were allowed to sign union cards.

These men and women, and many more, were often backed by black churches and relatively low-key civil rights groups. Even though their victories were small, they persevered.

"Or Does It Explode?"

Harlem Renaissance poet Langston Hughes told the nation in 1951 that if the American Dream was deferred for black people, it could "dry up like a raisin in the sun." Or, he warned, it could explode.

The barriers to decent living were affecting the ever-increasing number of black people making their exodus from the South. Hartford's black population had doubled in the fourteen years since the poet's prediction, from twelve thousand to twenty-five thousand in the summer of 1965. That year, a determined group of local leaders met with Hartford's commission on human relations in one more attempt to demand urgent government action. The National Association for the Advancement of Colored People (NAACP), the Catholic Interracial Council and the Congress on Racial Equality (CORE) once again laid out the problems facing the black community.

A young group of upstarts, the North End Community Action Program (NECAP), was also represented. Using the direct action techniques of the Student Nonviolent Coordinating Committee (SNCC) in the South, NECAP had recently earned its place at the civil rights table. At the March 11, 1965 meeting, the organizations reiterated to the city commission how there was no progress on Hartford's segregated schools, poor housing code enforcement or the pervasive job discrimination in both the public and private sectors. "Negroes are being deprived of basic rights," said one leader. There was a consensus among the groups that city hall's response to their concerns had been "a whitewash." After three hours of repeating the demands laid at the city's doorstep, the community leaders left frustrated and angry. "I hate to think of the demonstrations in Hartford which we're going to have if we don't get some action," said one member of the Catholic group.

CONFLICT AT CITY HALL

A few months later, as Watts, Chicago and other cities were burning, three hundred Hartford residents gathered in a north end parking lot. On the warm August night, NECAP director Charles Turner told the crowd that the uprisings in those cities were triggered by the same conditions Hartford's poor faced. One sign in the crowd read, "Turn Left or Be Shot." It was an order that the National Guard had just given to protest marchers in Watts, where martial law had been declared and dozens of black people had been killed.

The NECAP-led crowd then marched down Main Street to city hall. Thirty police officers had been bused in to meet them. As Turner and others attempted to bring a symbolic black coffin to the city hall steps, they were blocked by a line of police. After trying to cross the line and sit on the steps, Charles Turner and eight other marchers were arrested.

Word traveled fast through the north end that night. Soon, a crowd gathered at the original rally site. The police blocked access to the area. A few bottles and rocks were thrown into the streets, and fourteen more people were arrested. For the next five years, Connecticut cities braced for so-called race riots. Hartford's events were among the most widespread. On July 12, 1967, the arrest of a black teenager for allegedly swearing at a waitress triggered police brutality charges. Four nights of rock throwing, broken windows and arson ensued. One well-known black conservative blamed "engineers of violence" who were supposedly directing the street disturbances.

One of those "engineers" was twenty-two-year old David Bradshaw, who was randomly scooped up by police and thrown in Seyms Street Jail. Bradshaw had just come back from a southern voter registration drive. While at Seyms Street awaiting trial, he spent his time organizing inmates for a brief nonviolent strike to improve the filthy jail conditions.

Dr. Martin Luther King Jr. had an answer to those who condemned urban insurrections without bothering to look at the root of the problems: "It is not enough for me to stand before you tonight and condemn riots. It would be morally irresponsible for me to do that without, at the same time, condemning the contingent, intolerable conditions that exist in our society. These conditions are the things that cause individuals to feel that they have no other alternative than to engage in violent rebellions to get attention. And I must say tonight that a riot is the language of the unheard."

Less than a month later, on April 4, 1968, King was assassinated. He joined the list of martyrs, like Medgar Evers, Viola Liuzzo, Jimmie Lee Jackson, James Cheney, Andrew Goodman and Michael Schwerner—all nonviolent civil rights activists cut down by racist violence.

Those who stepped into the Hartford streets on subsequent nights were labeled a "mob." A walkout by 400 Hartford Public High School students was probably the largest spontaneous reaction to King's death, but it received only a fraction of the news coverage. A Weaver High march of 150 students down Albany Avenue reached Constitution Plaza, home of the chamber of commerce and the site of the displacement of hundreds of low-income families. Apparently, no news organization made the connection between the students' anger and their highly symbolic target. Earlier that year, the chamber had recommended a $3.5 million cut in the Hartford school budget.

The "Labor Day Riots" of 1969 began when a white motorcycle gang, disturbed by Puerto Rican families moving into their turf, harassed local Hispanics. From the community's perspective, the Hartford police were doing nothing to stop the gang's nightly raids.

From June to August, the police escalated their violent tactics in response to almost every "racial" situation. They began to carry shotguns, shooting at least two white bystanders by mistake. Police used tear gas and dogs to break up groups of young people. Teargas spread through nearby apartments. One police officer was injured by a gas canister shot by a fellow cop during the confusion.

Each police incident threw gasoline on the fire. Black youths, unemployed, fought back. As local NAACP president Wilber G. Smith had warned the chamber of commerce, there were three thousand businesses in Hartford offering a mere two hundred jobs to young people that summer.

From March to July 1970, five black or Puerto Rican men were killed by Hartford police. None of them were part of a riot. Gary Hansley and William Casey were both shot and killed in separate instances after being stopped for alleged minor offenses (a purse snatching, a traffic violation, respectively).

Abraham Rodriguez and Efraim Gonzalez were both unarmed when they were killed by police. Rodriguez was shot following a car chase. A coroner's investigation found the police officer criminally negligent. Gonzalez was killed by a "stray" police shotgun blast while he was walking with his brother. An eleven-year-old girl was also struck by shotgun fire that entered through her apartment window. After an admittedly "incomplete" police investigation, no officer was ever identified as the shooter.

An ad hoc group of seventy-eight Hartford-area Catholic priests and nuns condemned the killings, demanding a return to "human life taking precedence over property rights." Four decades later, a similar demand would be chanted in Ferguson, Missouri, after the 2013 fatal police shooting of eighteen-year-old Michael Brown: "Black Lives Matter."

THE BLACK PANTHERS

On May 1, 1969, Hartford mayor Ann Uccello was flanked by the city's chamber of commerce as she held up a broom on the city hall steps. This press photo-op was the chamber's annual Clean-Up Day: business and government united to inspire civic pride and personal responsibility among Hartford's residents.

Just one block away, at the same moment, the Black Panther Party had assembled dozens of young people at the Federal Building. The crowd marched, waved flags and chanted. The Panthers, who found fertile ground

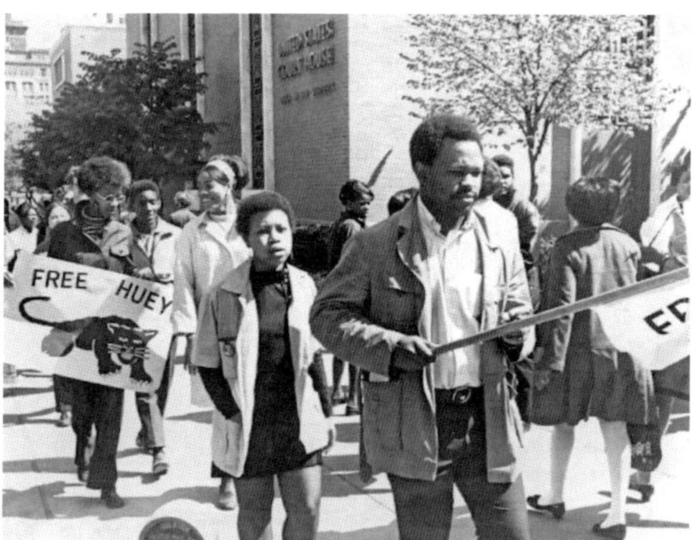

Black Panther rally at the Hartford Federal Building on Main Street, May 1, 1969. *Hartford History Center, Hartford Public Library.*.

for recruitment in Connecticut, did not carry brooms—or guns. The party was responding to poverty, violence and oppression in Hartford's black community. Their weapon of choice was a manifesto, the ten-point program entitled "What We Want/What We Believe."

The Black Panther program called for full employment, exemption from military service and the "immediate end to POLICE BRUTALITY and MURDER of Black people." The program was written in 1966 by founders Huey P. Newton and Bobby Seale in Oakland, California. They demanded "land, bread, housing, education, clothing, justice, and peace." The statement ended with the Declaration of Independence.

DIVIDED BY RACE AND CLASS

City hall, located in the city's center, was Hartford's dividing line in more ways than one. Downtown separated the black, poor north end from the stable, white working-class south end. The two areas reflected America's race and class divisions, particularly the wide gap between how Connecticut's black and white residents viewed the source of the 1960s urban rebellions.

The racial divide encompassed discrimination in jobs, housing and education. Police brutality ranked high on the black community's grievance list. A confidential analysis of Hartford police/community relations was released in June 1969. The timing was perfect: a citywide curfew, triggered by clashes between police and young black men, had just been lifted. The study was written by the respected criminal justice scholar Dr. Sol Chaneles at the behest of the local authorities. His "top secret report on crime in Hartford" showed that African Americans believed the Hartford police force spent more time "harassing ghetto residents" than protecting them. Dr. Chaneles, who had previously worked for the U.S. Chamber of Commerce, reported that the overwhelming percentage of major crimes in the city were committed by whites, not blacks or Puerto Ricans. Yet according to Chaneles's report, a "disproportionate amount of time was spent protecting downtown business establishments" from petty infractions. Meanwhile, a dozen organized crime rings operated freely in the city. Hartford's police chief denied every accusation.

WHO JOINED THE PANTHERS?

Walter "Rap" Bailey grew up in Hartford. He described how black youth from the projects experienced more violence and deprivation "than any child is meant to see." He was motivated to join the Panthers after marching with John Barber, leader of the Black Caucus. On September 18, 1967, Barber led three hundred people on an "open housing" march from the north end to south Hartford. Their target was the practice of segregated housing that made buying or renting homes in the south end practically impossible for African American families. The protesters were militant but peaceful. The group was integrated and included white students from the Community for Nonviolent Action (CNVA) in Voluntown.

The protesters were stopped by police before they reached downtown. Bottles and rocks were thrown into the street, but apparently not by the marchers. According to Bailey, police waded into the crowd, hitting and arresting people at random. One newspaper photo showed a tall, skinny white pacifist youth being manhandled by two officers. Word of the arrests spread; that night, Hartford experienced its first full-scale riot. When the Panthers started recruiting, Rap Bailey was among the first to join.

Charles "Butch" Lewis, a well-known and respected figure in the black community, helped organize the Black Panther Party in Hartford. Lewis grew up in the South, moved to Hartford, was drafted and served in Vietnam for fourteen months. As a veteran and a respected figure in the neighborhood, he was designated field captain.

Lewis understood white people's perception of the Panthers. "I know a lot of people fear we're a gang of thugs and hoodlums," he said during an early Panther demonstration. "But we're a political party, not a gang. We're an army of people who are fighting for the people, the oppressed people."

HISTORY OF SELF-DEFENSE

At a "Colored Men's Convention" in Hartford on January 26, 1899, Connecticut's first black lawyer took to the stage with an uncompromising message. "It is the right of the colored man to fight for his rights," Walter S. Miller told the crowd. "When a white man shows a revolver, I want the Negro to show one also. In that way only will he be granted his rights by demanding them and being ready to insist upon them."

African Americans have organized for self-defense since the Civil War. From the 1920s to the 1960s, Connecticut activists formed a number of membership groups to that end. The Anti-Lynching Crusaders (led by Mary Townsend Seymour), the Negro Defense Council and the Hartford League of Struggle for Negro Rights were just some of the organizations that protested police and vigilante violence on a local and national level.

In 1961, the U.S. Civil Rights Commission found that, as the civil rights movement grew, a majority of African Americans feared a racist backlash. They feared police violence and harassment, as well. The commission reported that when racial violence took place, the black community had come to expect that "the police will side with the white mob." The same report found that "Negroes feel the brunt of brutality proportionately more than other groups in American society."

When the Panthers took to the Hartford streets in the summer of 1969, their first priority was to "patrol the police." Panther leader Don Mounds told a public forum, "What we were doing was patrolling the police for the simple reason that we knew, like a lot of people know, that the police make false arrests, shoot tear gas into the houses. The police came into the area like storm troopers. We were threatened to be arrested and a few of us were arrested. We still did our thing, you know."

The Black Panther presence, and the party's use of the Second Amendment to carry arms, was seen by police force as a direct threat to its authority. Yet even when neighborhood groups attempted to protect black lives and property, they found their efforts blocked by the police department. The Oakland Civic Association formed an unarmed patrol of men to watch their neighborhood. This effort had some funding behind it; the men were equipped with berets, whistles and walkie-talkies. The Hartford police forced the patrol to abandon its berets and equipment, but disturbances dropped significantly while the community group was in the street.

SURVIVAL PROGRAMS

Throughout its brief existence in Connecticut (1969–72), the Black Panther Party prioritized community service. This was not service for its own sake, but "survival programs" undertaken while the Panthers were working to raise the political consciousness of people of color and the urban poor.

One of the most successful outreach efforts was the Panthers' free breakfast program for children. It won significant support from local grocery stores and individual donors. In Hartford, breakfast was served at St. Michael's Church on Clark Street. One of St. Michael's resident priests was Father Leonard Tartaglia, an outspoken critic of institutional racism and a close ally of the Panthers. Kids stopped by the Panthers' kitchen before school for breakfast and sometimes for clothing, as well. In many areas, Panthers provided medical and other services not available to low-income neighborhoods.

The Panthers also had other priorities. One of the most important was its newspaper, the *Black Panther*. All members were required to distribute it, and when they hit college campuses, sales were brisk. On Hartford streets, young Panthers were regularly arrested by the police for soliciting, only to have charges dropped immediately. Members like George Green (seventeen), Gwen Rhodes (sixteen) and Willie Ledbetter (fourteen) of Hartford were harassed and arrested. Declassified FBI documents have subsequently revealed that J. Edgar Hoover urged local police disruption of Panther newspaper production and sales.

LIFE OR DEATH

One example of Panther community service in Hartford stood above the rest, literally a matter of life or death. Hartford officials had promised the public housing tenants of Charter Oak Terrace in 1968 that the overflowing Park River would be fixed. The river had caused the drowning deaths of several children when the water rose to a dangerous level. In 1969, while the tenants were still waiting for action, another child drowned.

This time, the parents contacted the Black Panthers. Butch Lewis and Rap Bailey advised the parents as they picketed in the street, blocking traffic. The Hartford Police arrived to break up the nonviolent action and threaten arrests, but the parents pledged to come back the next day. Return they did, and the attention they attracted increased their numbers. The city inspected the bridge over the river and determined that it was in danger of collapse. Workers immediately erected a temporary buttress to stabilize the structure.

The Charter Oak neighbors met with Governor John Dempsey. Further river inspection showed that there was a blockage downstream that should have been dismantled several years earlier. The obstruction was removed, and the river's water was lowered to its normal, safe level of a few inches.

What none of the participants knew at the time was that the FBI was on the scene. Agents sent "Urgent" teletype memos directly to J. Edgar Hoover. Specifically because of the Panthers' involvement, the bureau feared "possible racial violence" (its words) because of this peaceful protest.

GOVERNMENT SPYING

From the beginning, the Panthers were spied upon by local police departments and the FBI. Hoover placed enormous emphasis on crushing the Black Panther Party and its programs. In Connecticut, the FBI used wiretapping and informers to prepare reports sent directly to the bureau chief. The effort was part of his secret (and often illegal) COINTELPRO operation, which a U.S. Senate investigation later exposed as "a sophisticated vigilante operation."

The Panthers were sure the police and feds were spying on them, but declassified files also show that the U.S. Army's 108th Military Intelligence group was watching. The army had a secret office in the Hartford Federal Building and shared its findings with other government agencies.

Were the Black Panthers heroes or villains? Hoover called them "the greatest threat to the internal security of the country." Dr. Cornel West, a leading African American scholar, credited the Panthers with "turning scared, intimidated, helpless folk into bold, brave, hopeful people willing to live and die for Black freedom."

TAKING SIDES

The city, and indeed the nation, has not reached consensus on either the causes or the solutions to urban revolts. Nowhere was this clearer than the polar opposite positions taken by Thomas J. Dodd and Abraham A. Ribicoff, Connecticut's two U.S. senators, both Democrats, in the 1960s.

Senator Ribicoff believed that the cause of riots stemmed from "100 years of neglect" of the black community. Senator Dodd called riots "an incipient civil war," with whites as the target.

Abe Ribicoff said, "Black Americans are now presenting the consequences to the nation" of that neglect. Tom Dodd insisted that riots were the work of "black extremists" who were controlled by Red China and Fidel Castro.

Ribicoff cited the $30 billion annual spending on the Vietnam War, which siphoned off badly needed funds for the cities. Dodd declared that the United States was "strong enough" to prosecute the war and run the country at the same time.

Senator Ribicoff pledged to submit a $1 trillion bill to fund a housing program and full employment. Senator Dodd authored "riot control" legislation that would increase the penalty to twenty years in prison for agitators who crossed a state line to incite a riot.

The two men, much like the rest of the nation, could not have been further apart.

BIBLIOGRAPHY

Some of the material in this book originally appeared on my website, www.ShoeleatherHistoryProject, or in articles I have written for connecticuthistory.org and ctmirror.org.

1. Prostitution, the Social Evil

Bridgeport Herald. "The State Police Have Marked Every Brothel in City of Hartford." October 1, 1905.

Goldman, Emma. *Marriage and Love*. New York: Mother Earth Publishing Association, 1911.

Hepburn, Katharine Houghton. *The White Slave Traffic in Hartford, Connecticut: Some Striking Examples of the Need of Votes for Women Taken from the Hartford Campaign Against Commercialized Vice*. Hartford: Connecticut Woman Suffrage Association, 1914.

Wells, Ernest Alden. *Report of the Hartford Vice Commission, Hartford, Conn.* Hartford, CT: Hartford Commission, 1913.

2. Wicked Sam Colt

Chaffin, Tom. *Fatal Glory: Narcisco Lopez and the First Clandestine US War against Cuba*. Charlottesville: University of Virginia Press, 1996.

Farrow, Anne, and Joel Lang. *Complicity: How the North Promoted, Prolonged and Profited from Slavery*. New York: Ballantine Books, 2006.

Grose, Francis. *Dictionary of the Vulgar Tongue*. 1811. Northfield, IL: Digest Books, 1971.

Hartford Courant. "Connecticut Legislature." June 20, 1861.

———. "The Fight." April 13, 1869.

———. "Letter to the Editor." Solomon Porter, September 19, 1853.

———. "Meeting at the City Hall Last Night, to Save the Union." December 15, 1859.

———. Untitled. March 14, 1882.

Hosley, William. *Colt: The Making of an American Legend*. Amherst: University of Massachusetts Press, 1996.

New York Times. "A Word to the People of Connecticut." January 14, 1861.

Phelps, M. William. *The Devil's Right Hand: The Tragic Story of the Colt Family Curse*. Guilford, CT: Lyons Press, 2013.

Schechter, Harold. *Killer Colt, Murder, Disgrace, and the Making of an American Legend*. New York: Ballantine Books, 2010.

Twain, Mark. Untitled article. *Hartford Courant*, October 12, 1874.

3. Hoboes, Tramps and Bums

Hartford Courant. "The Harvest of Tramps." January 30, 1875.

———. "John Smith, Tramp." August 21, 1899.

———. "Letters from the People: A Voice from the Tramps." October 15, 1875.

———. "Lodgers at the Station House." February 1, 1871.

———. "The Management of Tramps." March 10, 1879.

———. "Only a Pauper Whom Nobody Owns." February 15, 1875.

———. "The Progress of Poverty." April 30, 1875.

McCook, John J. "Leaves from the Diary of a Tramp." *Independent* 53, no. 2764 (November 21, 1901) and no. 2766 (December 5, 1901).

Ryan, Bill. "19th-Century Reformer's Way with the Homeless." *New York Times*, May 8, 1994.

4. The Scourge of Alcohol

Geer's Hartford Directory (Including West Hartford and East Hartford, Connecticut), 1899–1901. Hartford, CT: Hartford Printing Company.

Hartford Courant. "Battling Bootleggers, Rumrunners and Secret Supplies of Hooch." April 25, 2014.

———. "Brewers on Strike." April 11, 1900.

———. "Opium Smoking in Hartford: A Reporter Investigates One of the Dives Not Illegal, According to Laws of This State." January 31, 1907.

———. "A Report for Opium." March 9, 1909.

———. "Some Amazing Stories: Mexico Has Drugs of which Queer Things Are Said." January 30, 1905.

———. "The Use of Opium." March 11, 1884.

McDonald, Brian. *Indian Summer: The Tragic Story of Louis Francis Sockalexis, the First Native American Major League Baseball Player*. Emmaus, PA: Rodale Books, 2003.

5. Baby Farming in Hartford?

Cedar Hill Foundation. "Virginia Thrall Smith, (1836–1903)." Hartford, Connecticut. Cedar Hill Foundation.org.

Cohen, Linda Smith. Unpublished thesis, 1993. Quote of letter from Virginia Thrall Smith to Isabella Hooker.

Connecticut Women's Hall of Fame. "Virginia Thrall Smith." 1994. cwhf.org.

Cornelius, Barbara L. *History of Sunset Farm, 1867–1993*. West Hartford, CT: Sunset Farm Corporation, 1993.

Eagle, Mary Kavanaugh Oldham, ed. *The Congress of Women: Held in the Woman's Building, World's Columbian Exposition*. Chicago: Monarch Book Company, 1894.

Hartford Courant. "Cases of Diphtheria." October 27, 1891.

———. "City Briefs." April 9, 1884.

———. "City Government—Last Evening." May 10, 1864.

———. "Neglect of the Town Authorities." April 22, 1864.

———. "Nobody Wants Her." June 27, 1900.

———. "The Old Pest House Burned." July 6, 1885.

———. "One Case Temporarily Provided for—A Great Need Still Exists." December 25, 1883.

———. "Pest House." January 28, 1857.

———. "Smallpox Afloat." March 18, 1874.

———. "Some December Weather." December 24, 1883.

———. "Town Meeting." December 5, 1848, and August 18, 1849.

———. "Vaccination." February 5, 1857.

Herman, Ellen. *The Adoption History Project*. Department of History. University of Oregon. 2012. http://pages.uoregon.edu/adoption/index.html.

Leach, Eugene. "Connecticut's Philanthropic Impulse." Connecticut Explored. December 18, 2015. http://www.ctexplored.org.

Rosen, Dr. Bruce. "Baby Farming." Victorian History. March 14, 2012. www.vichist.blogspot.com.

"Neighborhood History; Asylum Hill." www.FarmingtonAvenue.org/html/hoodHistory.

Twain, Mark, and Harriet E. Smith, eds. *The Autobiography of Mark Twain: The Complete and Authoritative Edition*. Vol. 1. Oakland: University of California Press, 2010.

6. No Relief: Grinding Poverty in the Great Depression

Bucki, Cecelia. *Bridgeport's Socialist New Deal, 1915–36*. Urbana: University of Illinois Press, 2001.

Daily Alta California. "Letter from 'Mark Twain.'" September 6, 1868.

Hartford Courant. "Aviation Field City Workers Gain a Point: 'Strike' of Unemployed Against 'No Pay in Cash' Order Wins Concession of $1 a Day." August 6, 1931.

———. "Mayor Insists Air Terminal to Aid Idle: List of Available Skilled Workers Asked from Welfare Dept. After Open Shop Protest Praises Batterson's Aviation Field Plans." August 7, 1931.

———. "Welfare Board Supports Brainard Field Pay Policy: Commissioners Behind Proposal to Compensate Men with Rent, Supplies." August 9, 1931.

Piven, Francis Fox, and Richard A. Cloward. *Regulating the Poor: The Function of Public Welfare*. New York: Pantheon Books, 1971.

Twain, Mark, and Charles Dudley Warner. *The Gilded Age: A Tale of Today*. Hartford, CT: American Publishing Company, 1874.

Van Dusen, Albert E. *Connecticut*. New York: Random House, 1961.

Workers Age. "Fight Against Forced Labor! Hartford Association of Unemployed Leads Struggle against Mayor's Peonage Scheme." May 1, 1933.

7. David and Goliath: Birdsall vs. Bulkeley

Hartford Courant. "The Birdsall Affair." November 19, 1888.
———. "The Birdsall Cases End," March 14, 1889.
———. "Horsewhipped. Birdsall Severely Punished." November 17, 1888.
———. "Judge Henney Binds the Defendants Over to the Next Criminal Term of Superior Court." November 21, 1888.
Hartford History. "Mayors of Hartford." http://www.hartfordhistory.net/mayors.html.
Hartford Telegram. November 1887.
National Law Review no. 384 (1888).
Van Dusen, Albert E. *Connecticut*. New York: Random House, 1961.

8. Newsies, Bootblacks and Telegraph Boys

Hartford Courant. "Aldermen Hear Defense by Boot Black." July 20, 1930.
———. "Boot Blacks and Ragpickers." October 20, 1880.
———. "Boy Boot Black Philosophizes on Life Here." December 12, 1929.
———. "Boy Boot Black 'Station' Plan Is Suggested." July 14, 1932.
———. "The Italian Boot Blacks." September 12, 1900.
———. "News and Notions." November 20, 1875.
———. "Organized Labor." December 12, 1900.
———. "Rag Pickers, Boot Blacks." April 1, 1902.

9. Fascism in Fashion

Barrow, David J. *Liberty and Sexuality: The Right to Privacy and the Making of Roe v. Wade*. Oakland: University of California Press, 1998
DiMaggio, Paul J., ed. *Nonprofit Enterprise in the Arts: Studies in Mission and Constraint*. Cary, NC: Oxford University Press, 1986.
Hartford Courant. "Priest Lauds Organizing of Boys Brigade." March 8, 1937.
Karrer, Wolfgang. "Drastic Community: Wallace Stevens and Mussolini." 2009. http://www.wkarrer.webs.com.

10. Hell Hole: Seyms Street Jail

Brown, Rome G., Zechariah Chafee, Jr., Felix Frankfurter, Ernst Freund, Swineburne Hale, Francis Fisher Kane, Alfred S. Niles et al. *To the American People; Report Upon the Illegal Practices of the United States Department of Justice*. Washington, D.C.: National Popular Government League, 1920.

Fedorowich, Ed. *Steel-Bar Motel*. Lincoln, NE: Author's Choice Press, 2000.

Thornton, Steve. *A Shoeleather History of the Wobblies*. Boston: Red Sun Press, 2013.

11. Fales & Gray Catastrophe: Not Just an Accident

Hartford Courant. "100 Workers Are Dying Each Day." February 24, 1912.

Linder, Marc. "Fatal Subtraction: Statistical MIAs on the Industrial Battlefield." *Journal of Legislation*. Iowa City: University of Iowa, 1994.

Zinn, Howard. *A People's History of the United States, 1492–Present*. New York: Harper Collins, 1980.

12. Hartford's Original Sin

Baldwin, Peter C. *Domesticating the Street: The Reform of Public Space in Hartford, 1850–1930*. Columbus: Ohio State University Press, 1999.

Connecticut State Library. "Black Governors." http://www.cslib.org/gov/blackgov.htm.

Cruz, José E. *Identity and Power: Puerto Rican Politics and the Challenge of Ethnicity*. Philadelphia, PA: Temple University Press, 1998.

Dr. Huey P. Newton Foundation. *The Black Panther Party: Service to the People Programs*. Albuquerque: University of New Mexico Press, 2008.

Fabre, Geneviève et al. *Celebrating Ethnicity and Nation*. Heidelberg: Berghahn Books, 2001.

Fowler, William C., LLD. "The Historical Status of the Negro in Connecticut. A Paper Read Before the New Haven Colony Historical Society." Hathi Trust Digital Library.

Greene, Lorenzo Johnston. *The Negro in Colonial New England: 1620–1776*. New York: Columbia University Press, 1942.

Hartford History Center. "Butch Lewis Video Collection Documenting Civil Rights Era, Hartford." Hartford Public Library, 2014.

———. "Digital Collection: Hartford Times (1950–1976)—Reflection of the Times." Hartford Public Library, 2014.

Hartford News. "Black Governors Ball Saturday." April 25, 2007.

National Archives. Now online: 1,582 pages from FBI on Black Panther Party in Connecticut, courtesy of the National Archives. http://commons.trincoll.edu/jackdougherty/2014/03/05/fbi-black-panther/#sthash.iVRh00Ab.dpufhttp://commons.trincoll.edu/jackdougherty/2014/03/05/fbi-black-panther.

Newton, Huey P. *Revolutionary Suicide*. New York: Penguin Books, 1973.

Norton, Frederick Calvin. "Negro Slavery in Connecticut." *Connecticut* 5, no. 6 (1899).

Opdyck, Charles Wilson. *The Opdyck Genealogy*. 1889. Internet Archive. Boston Public Library, 2011.

Physicians for Human Rights. Examining Asylum Seekers: A Health Professional's Guide to Medical and Psychological Evaluations of Torture. August 2001.

Scaevas History. "Black Governors in Connecticut." http://freepages.genealogy.rootsweb.ancestry.com/~nyterry/towns/hartford/blackgoverners-sca.html.

Skolnick, Jerome, Hugh Davis Graham, Ted Robert Gurr, and Louis H. Mascotti. A Report to the National Commission on the Causes and Prevention of Violence. A Staff Report to the National Commission on the Causes and Prevention of Violence. Washington, DC: Government Printing Office, 1969.

Sterling, Dorothy. *Speak Out in Thunder Tones*. Cambridge, MA: DaCapo Press, 1998. This includes the one description I have found by Ebenezer Bassett, an African American who wrote a brief recollection of his father as a Negro Governor.

Thornton, Steve. "The Rise of the Black Panther Party in Connecticut." ConnecticutHistory.org.

United States Commission on Civil Rights. Justice. United States Commission on Civil Rights Report. Vol. 5. 1961. http://www.crmvet.org/docs/ccr_61_justice.pdf.

United States Senate. The FBI's Covert Program to Destroy the Black Panther Party. (pages 185- 223), Final Report of the Select Committee to Study Governmental Operations with Respect to Intelligence Activities. April. 23, 1976. https://archive.org/stream/finalreportofsel03unit#page/184/mode/2up.

ABOUT THE AUTHOR

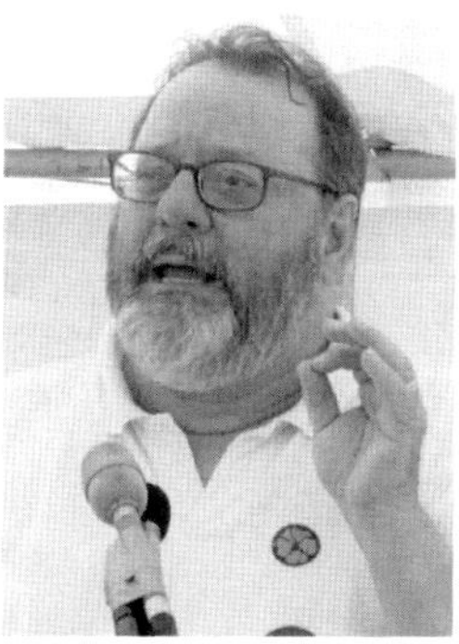

Steve Thornton is the creator of The Shoeleather History Project, which documents and explores stories from Hartford's grass roots. He maintains a website, leads workshops and conducts interactive walking tours that feature ordinary people who are the real makers of history.

Steve has been an activist and organizer all his life and retired in 2013 as a vice president of District 1199/SEIU, Connecticut's largest healthcare union. He is a member of the National Writers Union and the IWW.

In his capacity as an educator, Steve has engaged more than 2,500 rank-and-file healthcare workers through popular education to become workplace union leaders. He has also trained hundreds of people from Vermont to Georgia in nonviolent direct action. He regularly speaks to students at elementary schools, high schools and universities, as well as to historical societies and activist groups.

Steve is the author of *A Shoeleather History of the Wobblies: Stories of the Industrial Workers of the World (IWW) in Connecticut* (Red Sun Press, 2013).